MICHELANGELO

Michelangelo Buonarroti, possibly a self-portrait (Casa Buonarroti, Florence)

IMMORTALS OF ART

MICHEL-ANGELO

by Monroe Stearns

FRANKLIN WATTS, INC.
575 Lexington Avenue
New York, N.Y. 10022

SBN 531 00944–0

Copyright © 1970 by Franklin Watts, Inc.
Library of Congress Catalog Card Number: 78–95640
Printed in the United States of America

CONTENTS

	PREFACE: MICHELANGELO TODAY	vii
I	THE HILLS AND THE PLAIN	3
II	THE PALACE AND THE CHURCH	13
III	FLIGHT AND FAME	31
IV	HONOR AT HOME	53
V	PRISONERS IN STONE	79
VI	THE POPE AND THE PAINTER	97
VII	THE TORMENTS OF TIME	125
VIII	THOUGHT AND ACTION	141
IX	DAYS OF RECKONING	175
X	FROM CARVING TO BUILDING	195
XI	JOURNEY INTO THE FUTURE	219
	CHRONOLOGY	229
	BIBLIOGRAPHY	237
	INDEX	241

PREFACE: MICHELANGELO TODAY

Over four hundred years have gone by since Michelangelo Buonarroti died in Rome a few weeks before his eighty-ninth birthday. During that time the God-centered world he knew and accepted as a child has changed to a man-centered world in which "God is dead" seems to be a prominent philosophy.

Today artists in all fields interpret man as puny, if not deformed; as a helpless non–hero, fragmented and unhappy; passive; noble only in his capacity for endurance. To such an existential creature, God, if thought about at all, appears as an escapist myth created out of man's own sense of despair and futility. Hence the contemporary artist's tone is compassionate; a challenging or inspirational one seems heartless. Such attitudes Michelangelo would have found abhorrent.

It may seem difficult, therefore, to appreciate the meaning for the present time of Michelangelo's emphatic statements in his art that man is the image and likeness of God, and to understand Michelangelo's representations of God as primal, the essence of dynamic power, the giver and ruler of life.

Michelangelo's long lifetime, however, encompassed the beginnings of that change. As a thinking, feeling person, he had first to cope with the newly discovered philosophy of the ancient Greeks, which demonstrated to him that revelation of the nature of God and man was not confined to the Judeo-Christian tradition alone. He saw the tiny known world expand into one almost as large as the one we know today. He witnessed the destruction of the unity of Christian faith by the Protestant Reformation. He had to accept the proof that this planet is not the hub of the universe, but only a tiny element in its periphery. Because they were new, these revolutionary conceptions forced upon Michelangelo a greater adjustment than their derivatives have imposed upon the present generation of men who have grown used to them.

Michelangelo's works are his spiritual biography. In them can be seen exactly how one man dealt with a world he saw shattering around him and becoming well-nigh incomprehensible. In Michelangelo's development of thought from the bold, aggressive, heroic *David* of his early years to the poignantly tragic resignation of his last work, the *Rondanini Pietà*, is the dynamic progression of a very human being whose unconquerable faith was that man is only "a little lower than the angels." Michelangelo's work demonstrates that this estimate of man by the Psalmist of old—perhaps Michelangelo's favorite human character—is as true today as it was in the fifteenth and sixteenth centuries.

Many principles of living can be abstracted from Michelangelo's long experience. Perhaps the one most appealing to persons caught in the complexity of twentieth-century existence is simplification. Baffled and tormented by conflicting systems of philosophy, and by conflicting demands upon his time and his skill, he determined to concentrate his energies on only those ideas and activities that had a true meaning for him as an individual—what, in contemporary slang, might be called "his own thing." He disciplined himself to discard whatever was inconsequential or irrelevant in that regard. His work illustrates the great principle of all art—whether the art of living or the art of interpreting life—"When in trouble, simplify." Such self-discipline, the only effective form of discipline, is a dimension of genius.

Genius, the one means by which mortal man may cross the chasm between the limited actual world and the limitless ideal world, may be partially defined as imagination disciplined into communicable form. No artist has ever mastered this aspect of genius to a greater degree than Michelangelo. His soaring thought, expressed in simple form—for none of his masterpieces is in itself complicated—reaches across the gap of four hundred years to say what he himself knew, namely, that man and God need not be divided.

The scope of this account does not permit much consideration of the unclear aspects of Michelangelo's life and works. An absence of facts permits only guesswork about some parts of his life. This writer believes that his own guesswork can contribute nothing to the enormous mass of conflicting opinions that already exists, and so has omitted any lengthy discussion of the pros and cons. Similarly, comment on those works of Michelangelo's that have not been completely authenticated, or are clearly not principally from Michelangelo's own hands, has been omitted from the text, and such works are not illustrated.

The number of illustrations has had to be curtailed for the same reason. To reproduce the entire ceiling of the Sistine Chapel, for example, not to mention showing details of it, would require a book far larger than this one. Such books do exist, however, and are well worth the reader's time and effort —providing he cannot see the work itself. The same is true of other works of Michelangelo, particularly the sculpture. Just as no color reproduction can adequately convey the vibrant luminosity of Michelangelo's paintings, so no black and white, or even tinted, photograph can even imply the marvelous translucency and sheen of Michelangelo's marbles and their variety of texture. Nor can they indicate the size and context of his architectural work.

The reader, therefore, is urged to be tolerant of the gulf between this representation of Michelangelo's life and works and the real thing—just as Michelangelo eventually came to accept the tragedy of not being able to make his hands do all that his stupendous mind commanded them to do.

MONROE STEARNS

Tuscany, Rome, New York

MICHELANGELO

I: THE HILLS AND THE PLAIN

Toward the end of September in the year 1474, Lodovico Buonarroti, the younger son of an impoverished family, set out on horseback from the plain of Florence to cross the mountains of the central part of the Italian peninsula. His destination was the remote hill town of Caprese, about sixty miles east of Florence, the capital of the region known as Tuscany.

With Lodovico were his twenty-year-old wife Francesca and their son Lionardo, a year and a half old. Francesca was about four months pregnant. The journey was hard for her—all travel in those times was far from comfortable—and once she fell, or was thrown, from her horse, an accident from which she seems never to have fully recovered. But the misery of the trip probably meant little to the family, for at its conclusion the thirty-year-old Lodovico was to enter upon the honorific position of *podestà*, or city manager, of Caprese.

Actually the honor was more in the mind of Lodovico Buonarroti than in the office itself. Caprese, in the diocese of Arezzo, was not so much a town as a community of tiny villages. (Today Caprese has around two hundred inhabitants.) Lodovico's "invitation" to be its manager was the result of his long

petitioning of the *signoria* (city council) of Florence for some
political office worthy of his sense of his own importance.

The Buonarroti family had been taxpaying citizens of Florence for over three hundred years. They said—and Lodovico
insisted—that they were connected by blood with the counts of
Canossa, but that claim to nobility existed also only in Lodovico's imagination. This dream of lofty lineage compensated
him for his lowly position.

The family had been merchant bankers, but their small
business had reached the verge of bankruptcy as a result of
mismanagement by Lodovico's father. His older brother Francesco, the real head of the family, was called a banker out of
courtesy, but he was little more than a money changer. The
family, however, enjoyed a certain respect—in the past, a few
had been members of the signoria—but it was a respect probably mixed with pity. Florence was an enormously rich city, and
wealth was its only real standard of social prestige.

Lodovico undoubtedly felt the sting of this pity, but he was
unable to do anything to remedy it. In the small circle of
respectable Florentines—the city numbered only some ninety
thousand inhabitants—he certainly would have heard of the
patronizing remark that the boss of Florence's leading political
party, Lorenzo de' Medici, made about him: "Lodovico Buonarroti will always be poor."

The shrewd Lorenzo de' Medici was clearly aware of the
inadequacies of the pathetic Lodovico Buonarroti. Probably
Lorenzo authorized the "invitation" to Lodovico to be podesta
of Caprese more to be free for a while of Lodovico's tedious
office-seeking than to reward the support of a capable and
valuable constituent.

The rough gray stone castle of Caprese, which was already
partially in ruins, sits on the summit of a hill two thousand feet
above sea level. The hill rises abruptly and steeply from a valley

of the Apennines, where the Arno River begins its course toward Florence and, eventually, the sea. Its battlements look out over the tops of oak, poplar, sycamore, and locust trees toward the craggy mountaintops. The air is crystal clear and invigorating.

Lodovico settled his household in a two-story stone house within the walls of the castle. The lower floor consisted of a single room with a vaulted ceiling. The upper floor, reached by an outside staircase, contained two rooms. In the smaller of these Francesca Buonarroti gave birth to her second son early in the morning of Monday, March 6, 1475.

His father immediately gave the infant the name of Michelangelo, a new one in the family. Two days later it was confirmed at the child's baptism in Caprese's little one-room stone church of San Giovanni (St. John), halfway down the hill from the castle. In honor of that event the town enlarged its name in 1964, the four-hundredth anniversary of Michelangelo Buonarroti's death, to Caprese Michelangelo.

Three weeks after the baptism, Lodovico Buonarroti had to move his family back to Florence. A podesta's term of office was usually one year, but Lodovico's was only six months. It expired on April 1, 1475. Some men made a kind of career of being podesta in one city or another year after year. Lodovico, however, got no other political "invitation" for thirty-five years, an indication that he could not have been very efficient in handling the affairs of diminutive Caprese.

Lodovico moved in with his brother. They had a doubtful title to a four-story, tawny stucco house in Florence, now Number 15 Via Anguillara, at the corner of Via Torta. It is in the Santa Croce (Holy Cross) parish of Florence, then—and now—a shabby and unfashionable section of the lively, splendid city. Francesco Buonarroti's wife Cassandra had brought him a generous dowry, the income from which probably paid most of the bills for the joint households. There must have been a certain amount of discord in that living arrangement, as there usually is in an establishment run by two women. The younger and poorer of these, Michelangelo's mother, was undoubtedly kept subordinate to her childless sister-in-law.

Francesca Buonarroti's family, however, kept increasing. In 1477, Buonarroto arrived, followed by Giovan Simone in 1479, and Sigismondo (called, for short, Gismondo), in 1481. Then Francesca died, possibly of complications in the birth of her youngest son.

The six-year-old Michelangelo had probably not seen much of his mother. Since Francesca was unable to nurse her second son, Michelangelo was entrusted to a foster-mother in Settignano, a village on a hilltop about three miles east of Florence, where Lodovico owned a small farm.*

This woman was the daughter of a stonecutter and the wife of another. Most of the people of Settignano worked in the stone quarries of the region, extracting rough chunks of soft gray rock that they would shape into useful blocks in their yards. "I drew in the chisel and the mallet with which I carve statues together with my mother's milk," Michelangelo later told his friend, pupil, and biographer Giorgio Vasari.

That humorous remark implies that Michelangelo may have spent a good deal of time with his foster-mother in rural Settignano, fascinated by the work of the stonecutters. At any rate, he seems to have been neglected by his own family.

Lodovico Buonarroti remarried in 1485. Even less is known of Michelangelo's stepmother Lucrezia than of his mother. Apparently she brought some order into the family she ac-

* The present Villa Michelangelo, Number 67 Via della Capponcina, Settignano, occupies the site of that home of Lodovico Buonarroti. The house, however, has been enlarged and beautified, and much of the farmland converted into handsome gardens. It is a private residence.

quired, for at least Michelangelo was sent to school shortly after her arrival. He was then four years past the average age at which Florentine boys began their education. In the meantime Florence itself had been his school.

For the previous two hundred years Florence had been the richest and most powerful city of western Europe. Florence's wealth and power came primarily from its trade and its silk and wool factories. It was also the banking center of Europe. The gold florin of Florence was the monetary standard of the time.

In the fifteenth century Florence was more than a city, it was a city-state. As such it dominated the smaller cities of Tuscany —Arezzo, Livorno, Lucca, Pisa, Pistoia, and lesser towns—an area of nearly nine thousand square miles. Italy at that time was merely a geographical expression; it would not be a unified nation for almost four hundred years.

Of all the many other city-states of the peninsula only Venice was a republic like Florence. Long ago the Florentine bankers and merchants had determined that none of their wealth was to be drained away in arbitrary tribute to a feudal tyrant. It was to be used entirely for the benefit of their own city-state. To that end they had set up and scrupulously maintained a relatively democratic system of government.

Naturally that system meant the existence of at least two political parties. One was that of the old feudal nobles, the landholders; the other, that of the merchants, traders, and bankers. For about seventy-five years various heads of the enormously rich banking family of the Medici had dominated the latter faction. In 1469 the twenty-year-old Lorenzo de' Medici inherited that leadership.

Lorenzo was called *il Magnifico* (the Magnificent), then a common term of respect and admiration. Still, in its modern sense, it could easily be applied to Lorenzo's character and his way of life. His only political office was equivalent to that of a

secretary of state or minister of foreign affairs in a modern
democracy. As such he was legally subject to the decrees of the
signoria, which was elected by the taxpaying citizens. That
body, however, knew better than to challenge his authority as
boss of the party in power, and so Lorenzo de' Medici was the
unofficial ruler of Florence.

Lorenzo the Magnificent performed his diplomatic assignments with superlative skill. Although he did divert tax moneys
to his own purposes and plunder a city fund, he was far less
corrupt and tyrannical a ruler than most of the despots who
governed the other city-states of Italy.

For three generations the Medici not only had been public-
spirited citizens of Florence, but had stimulated and patronized
the art and learning that made Florence the intellectual capital
of Europe. Lorenzo de' Medici continued and enlarged that
family tradition. In the sumptuous palace built by his grandfather on the Via Larga (Via Cavour, as it is known today) he
assembled scholars, poets, painters, sculptors, and architects
whom he regarded as members of his family. Himself a credit-
able poet, he took pleasure in listening to their discourses and
admiring the works of their hands. He was a physically ugly
man, but he possessed great charm, shrewdness, practicality,
and friendliness. Unpretentious, he made a point of knowing
by name all his political constituents, including Lodovico Buonarroti, and he took a sincere interest in their welfare.

During those three generations Florence had nourished and
employed most of the painters, sculptors, and architects whose
works are the glory of the period called the Early Renaissance in
Italy. A convenient date for the beginning of that epoch is the
year 1294, when the building of Florence's beautiful Duomo
(cathedral) commenced. From that time on, Florence had been
transforming itself from a medieval city with a medieval point
of view into a community whose buildings reflected the virtual

worship of man as a worthy individual. Hence the spirit of the Renaissance—humanism.

Humanism means faith in the value and the achievements of the individual human being, and joy in the world of nature and of man. It came from the rediscovery of the pagan spirit of the classic era of ancient Rome and of ancient Greece. The revival of this exuberant attitude invigorated the citizens of a democratic and competitive city like Florence, and made their talents flourish.

Michelangelo was born as this productive spirit was reaching its peak. The period of his lifetime, therefore, is known as the High Renaissance.

At the age of ten, Michelangelo was the equivalent in experience of a fifteen- or sixteen-year-old city boy of today. Life-spans were apt to be short in the fifteenth century, and men matured early. Furthermore, neglect had made Michelangelo independent. Because of his unorganized, motherless home life, he had to find a place for himself. Lacking a secure family as a social anchor, he had drifted into the life of the streets. This compelled him to rely for survival on whatever individual talents he had. Also it brought him into association with older boys with whom he had to compete or to whom he attached himself. Short and stocky and strong, he found the use of his fists the best way to drive home the opinions he expressed all too freely as a defense of his youth and his feelings of insecurity.

Thus he earned a certain respect from his companions. The experience, however, gave him an unduly aggressive personality. For most of his life he was quick to take offense, overprotective of his own safety, and violently outspoken. These qualities tended to hide his craving for kindness from others. When he found it, he became almost a slave to anyone who showed him love and admiration.

One can imagine Michelangelo at this time of his life protecting not only himself but also his next younger brother Buonarroto, who probably tagged along after him. Michelangelo felt very close to that brother, and remained devoted to him until Buonarroto died at the age of fifty-one. In his fondness for Buonarroto and his concern for his other younger brothers Michelangelo expressed his sense of missing the loving attention he expected from his parents. Throughout his long life as a single and often lonely man, Michelangelo showed much tender, protective affection for younger men.

Three years in Francesco da Urbino's elementary school were Michelangelo's only formal education. The schoolmaster was learned in grammar—the vocabulary, the syntax, and the stylistic use of language—and managed to awaken Michelangelo's interest in that discipline sufficiently for him to master it. Urbino showed the boy that in grammar was the basis of communication, the means by which he could effectively transmit his own ideas to other persons. Communication was a great need for the neglected lad, whose mind was already constructing a systematic world of its own to replace the disorder of his home life. He learned to understand the importance of organized communication to his survival as an individual.

Otherwise Michelangelo seems to have learned little in school, not even Latin, the universal language of the times. He had started school too late to be willingly subject to classroom discipline. He had already found another method of communication—drawing.

For in his independent and pugnacious life in the streets Michelangelo had gained the respect of an older boy, Francesco Granacci, who has been remembered for nearly five hundred years for few other reasons than that he set Michelangelo Buonarroti on the road to art. Granacci himself, however, became a competent but distinctly minor painter.

Granacci was an apprentice in the large art studio of the

three Ghirlandaio brothers, of whom Domenico was by far the most gifted painter. Like any other apprentice in that workshop, Granacci had been rigorously drilled in draughtsmanship. When Michelangelo saw his friend's drawings, his compulsive competitiveness drove him to equal them. He had found it easy to guide his pen in the shaded lines of Italian handwriting; now he found that he could expand those lines to reproduce the forms of nature and to shade them so that they acquired depth and meaning.

Suddenly the boy discovered that he could create an approximation of life itself on what had been previously only a blank wall. For, according to legend, he began his drawing on the walls of his father's villa in Settignano, where he executed an awesome head of a satyr. (The drawing now there, however, is obviously of a later date, if by Michelangelo at all.)

The thrill of creativity and Granacci's admiration led Michelangelo to cover the paper he was given for his school exercises with drawings, thereby undoubtedly earning for himself several cuffs or canings from his teacher. It also led him to desert his schoolmates, who were younger than he anyway, for the companionship of Francesco Granacci, who was sixteen years old in 1485, and of Granacci's fellow apprentices. Doubtless Michelangelo often played hooky from Urbino's school in order to follow these youths about Florence as they studied and copied the works of the masters in the city's churches. At any rate, Michelangelo was frequently scolded and beaten in what passed for his home whenever his truancy was reported to his father.

Granacci became fond of Michelangelo because of the younger boy's response to his influence and instruction. Determined to develop Michelangelo's obvious talent, he would bring him drawings from the Ghirlandaio workshop so that Michelangelo could copy them. Probably Granacci showed Michelangelo's adaptations of these drawings to his master, Domenico Ghirlandaio. Promptly Ghirlandaio moved to get this prodigy into his workshop before a rival painter took him on. Michelangelo lost no time in informing his father of Ghirlandaio's offer and of his own intention and determination to become an artist.

Lodovico Buonarroti was almost insane with disappointment at that news. It was already clear to him that his oldest son, Lionardo, would enter the Church and withdraw from worldly affairs, as he did in 1491. Thus, the responsibility of heading the family in the next generation would devolve upon Michelangelo. For the future head of his family to be an artist depressed the pitifully proud Lodovico.

An artist, however much his work might be admired, was ranked in Florentine society as a craftsman, a worker. Lodovico considered work beneath the dignity of a Buonarroti; he himself preferred genteel poverty. The fury of the father, who found an ally in his brother, made the already hellish household intolerable for Michelangelo. He was devoted to his father and grieved that his nature was compelling him to go against Lodovico's wishes. But the boy would not give in to the parental and avuncular pressure, which was physical as well as mental.

Eventually Lodovico Buonarroti, probably out of exhaustion, gave in. On April 1, 1488, he apprenticed the rebellious Michelangelo to Domenico Ghirlandaio and his brother David for three years. The boy was "to learn the art of painting"—so says the contract—"and to practice the same." The Ghirlandaios were to pay him twenty-four florins during the three years. On April 16, Michelangelo received his first compensation as an artist—two of the florins he had been promised.

II: THE PALACE AND THE CHURCH

In 1488 the major project of Domenico Ghirlandaio was the frescoing, with the help of the students in his workshop, of the apse of Florence's Church of Santa Maria Novella (New St. Mary's). Ghirlandaio was less a creative artist than a technically proficient—one might even say, "slick"—illustrator. The scenes from the life of the Virgin and of St. John the Baptist with which he was decorating the walls and the ceiling of the apse are really documentaries of Florentine daily life, especially that of the Tornabuoni family who had commissioned the frescoes. Ghirlandaio was unable even to suggest that the members of that family who appear as the actors in the sacred pageant had identified with the biblical characters they portray.

There was, however, no better place for an apprentice to learn the technique of fresco painting than Ghirlandaio's studio. During the year or more he spent in that workshop, Michelangelo seems to have mastered that technique sufficiently to be allowed to work on the Tornabuoni frescoes. In two of the scenes, "The Baptism of Christ" and "The Dormition of the Virgin," are figures probably executed by Michelangelo alone.

Already Michelangelo had developed an artist's penetrating eye and sound taste. He could both see and feel the inadequacies in Ghirlandaio's work—trite composition and an inability to transform models into the characters they were costumed to portray. Instead, therefore, of imitating his official master, Michelangelo went to the far greater masters of an earlier period of Florentine painting, principally to Giotto and Masaccio. Two of Michelangelo's early drawings are adaptations of figures by those masters.

Another powerful influence on the young Michelangelo was ancient sculpture. Many examples of the crude but expressive sculpture of the Etruscans and of adaptations from Greek sculpture by the more sophisticated ancient Romans existed in Florence. More of these were being discovered almost daily as the Florentine magnates excavated old sites in order to build their new palaces. Probably Michelangelo had read or had been told about the essays of Leon Battista Alberti, the great pioneer of Renaissance architecture, who wrote: "He who wishes to acquire a knowledge of form should draw from sculpture rather than from paintings."

Michelangelo followed that advice, and practiced to adapt the volume he perceived in three-dimensional sculptured forms to drawing and painting. Hence his work in those two-dimensional fields early acquired a massive quality that gives it power and intensity. As a result of Michelangelo's study of sculpture, his drawings of this period begin to show an expansion of the heroic simplicity he had learned from Giotto and Masaccio into full-bodied action. He acquired an ability to transform linear outlines into solid forms. This added to his drawn and painted figures a quality of spirit that makes them dynamically alive.

Ascanio Condivi, the other (with Giorgio Vasari) contemporary biographer of Michelangelo, said of him that he "had a very retentive memory . . . so that although he painted many thousands of figures, he never made one which resembled another or which was placed in the same attitude." Condivi was to become Michelangelo's pupil and knew him well, and Michelangelo told him a great deal about himself. "I have heard him say," Condivi adds, "that he never drew a line which he did not remember."

Vasari, in his own biography of Michelangelo, says that "when he saw others' works, he retained them completely, and used them so that nobody ever became aware." Whenever Michelangelo "copied"—and he did adapt other artists' ideas— he interpreted: that is, he learned to speak the language of art in his own accents. Also, early in his career, he found drawing and painting a means of expressing and communicating his feelings.

Words themselves merely describe. A poet selects and combines words which appeal to his readers' senses of sight and sound and awaken the reader's own memories. A composer relies on sound and rhythm to stimulate the listener's emotions so that they will respond to the composer's feelings about his subject. A painter expands communication by line and color and form. The sculptor uses form as his language. As poet, painter, and sculptor, Michelangelo had less regard for subject matter—the literal words of language—than for the unspoken and unspeakable dimensions of communication, the feelings aroused by the subject which give meaning rather than mere description or definition.

This perception of fuller communication, and Michelangelo's extraordinary ability to realize in concrete form what he had perceived as an abstraction, made his teachers into his pupils. Granacci, for example, who had taught Michelangelo how to use color, began to adapt Michelangelo's discoveries into his own work—so much so that at least one painting of Granacci's was for a long time thought to be by Michelangelo. The same is true of several other associates of Michelangelo at the beginning of his career. Later Michelangelo's work became so powerfully individualized that it could be only feebly imitated.

Although Ghirlandaio did not follow any of his remarkable apprentice's innovations, he was proud of having Michelangelo as his pupil. He recommended him, along with Granacci, as the best of his students to Lorenzo the Magnificent, probably in the summer of 1489.

The two young artists were, therefore, admitted to the academy which Lorenzo the Magnificent was establishing as his way of continuing the Medici patronage of art in Florence. In the center of the public park that Lorenzo's grandfather had created for his fellow citizens on the present Piazza San Marco (St. Mark's Square) was the pavilion that housed the Medici collection of ancient gems. Lorenzo added to this collection many casts of antique statues. From time to time there were also exhibited in the garden works by more recent sculptors such as Donatello and Pollaiuolo. All these works could serve as models for the sculptors Lorenzo wished to encourage, for he feared that with the removal from Florence to Venice of Donatello's chief pupil, Andrea Verocchio, the art of sculpture might become extinct in Florence.

The custodian of the collection, who was also to be in charge of the school that Lorenzo was founding, was Giovanni di Bertoldo, who had been a pupil of the great Donatello. Under Bertoldo, who was already too old to work at sculpture himself, Michelangelo learned the rudiments of modeling in clay and carving in stone.

Sculpture, which previously Michelangelo had merely observed, now became of greater importance to him as a means of expression than drawing and painting. The three major forms of art fused for Michelangelo into what he would later call his *disegno*, that is, his highly individualistic language of expression. To Michelangelo this meant the expression in plastic form of an entire idea—subject matter plus the artist's feelings about it. It included not only the literal drawing and modeling but the composition as well. For the arrangement of a subject, whether it is a single item or made up of several separate items, is an important dimension of the total meaning.

A furious energy, wholly concentrated on driving toward a goal, seems to have activated the young, vigorous Michelangelo. In an astonishingly short time he mastered the technique of cutting into stone. From an old block of marble he carved the head of a satyr which attracted the admiration of Lorenzo the Magnificent as he was inspecting the work of his protegés.

What caught Lorenzo's attention was the individual touch that Michelangelo had given his version of some ancient piece of sculpture. He had hollowed out the mouth, and given the satyr a tongue and a full set of teeth.

Lorenzo laughed good-humoredly. "But you should have known," he said to the boy, "that old folk never have all their teeth. There are always some missing."

After his patron had moved on, Michelangelo knocked out one of the satyr's teeth and dug into the marble gum in such a way that it looked as if the tooth had fallen out. Lorenzo returned and saw the improvement, and laughed again at the young sculptor's cleverness.

If that pleasant story is true, it is the only record of Michelangelo's ever having taken criticism gracefully. That winter, when the weather prevented the students from working in the open garden, Bertoldo sent them to the Church of the Carmines to copy Masaccio's dramatic frescoes in its Brancacci Chapel which were teaching, and were to teach, all the great masters who came after Masaccio. One of the boys, Pietro Torrigiano, three years older than Michelangelo, ventured to criticize Michelangelo's work. As he had learned to do in the streets of Florence, Michelangelo looked to his fists to defend his pride. But he underestimated his opponent. Torrigiano smashed his own fist into Michelangelo's face and broke his nose.

Torrigiano, as might be expected, told a different version of the story, for some say that he was banished from Florence for initiating an attack on the young genius. But Torrigiano did admit that "this mark of mine he will carry to the grave."

Michelangelo, who was not good-looking anyway, probably suffered more than physical pain from the blow. Possibly it increased his sense of being unloved, and made him even more withdrawn. His now increased ugliness also possibly strengthened his conception of ideal physical beauty, greater than any other artist's, and made the expression of that beauty a goal toward which Michelangelo strove as if to compensate for his own lack of it.

Actually Michelangelo had learned to model clay figures from imitating the more experienced Torrigiano, who became a fine sculptor himself. History, however, somewhat unfairly remembers Pietro more for having been the fellow who broke Michelangelo's nose.

Bertoldo was a perfectionist, and, like his master Donatello, insisted on the importance of drawing, even above modeling, as a preparation for sculpture. These principles he did instill, or at least reinforce, in Michelangelo. But Michelangelo's real teachers were the ancient sculptors whose works, both actual and in reproduction, he found in the Medici sculpture garden.

Lorenzo the Magnificent did not forget the independent young sculptor who had adjusted the satyr's expression to please his patron. Probably in the spring of 1490, Lorenzo invited Lodovico Buonarroti to the Medici palace and asked him to allow his gifted son to join the Medici household.

In spite of Lodovico's hope that Michelangelo would have a conventional education as a gentleman's son, the snobbish father could not resist this offer from the unofficial king of

Florence. After Lorenzo offered Lodovico a post in the customs office, and promised to pay Michelangelo five ducats a month so that the young artist could help his father out financially, Lodovico Buonarroti consented.

Thereupon Michelangelo moved from the crowded Buonarroti house in the shabby Santa Croce quarter to a room of his own in the gorgeous Medici palace. He ate at Lorenzo the Magnificent's own table along with Lorenzo's sons, Piero, Giovanni, and Giuliano, who were around his own age and who accepted him as a companion with the same respect their father showed him as an ornament of the Florentine state. Lorenzo gave Michelangelo a violet cloak as a tribute to his talents. In the society of that time it was a gift far more significant of esteem than a similar present would be today.

Both for his personal pleasure and for the protection and encouragement of learning and art in Florence, Lorenzo the Magnificent had gathered under his spacious roof the most gifted men of his time. The principal ones were (in order of their age) the translator and interpreter of Plato and his followers, Marsilio Ficino; the poet and professor of literature, Angelo Poliziano; and one of the intellectual prodigies of all time, Giovanni Pico della Mirandola. The capacities and achievements of these men still stagger the mind.

The diversion of the Medici household was to listen to those intellectual giants expound the Latin classics and particularly the recently rediscovered Greek ones, and to discuss the spirit of these ancient works with the scholars. For within Lorenzo the Magnificent's lifetime there had been opened up new and vast perspectives into the nature of man. Examining these became the intellectual preoccupation of the times. The frontiers of the human mind expanded as dramatically as man's actual penetration into space has since enlarged them.

The revelation of the thinking of the Greek philosopher

Plato introduced practically a new religion to the Florentine intellectuals. The core of this philosophy is Plato's distinction between the world of things existing in a space-time relationship and the world of ideas unlimited by the human measurement of space and time. The world of things can be perceived only through the human senses; the world of ideas is perceived by the mind of man. The world of supposedly real things is only an insubstantial shadow cast by the truly real ideas that exist in a world free of the limitations of time and space—hence pure and immortal. Man's earthly existence, with his soul confined in a physical, mortal body, is therefore a term of imprisonment from which he gains parole insofar as he directs his conduct by believing in the truth of the ideal rather than the falseness of the actual.

By translation Marsilio Ficino made available to western Europeans the works of Plato and Plato's much later followers known as the Neoplatonists. The emphasis in this entire body of thought is on the immortality of the soul. The human soul occupies a central position in the universe of those philosophers. The soul returns to God through contemplation of the ideal. The liberation of the immortal individual soul from its mortal prison, then, is the aim of this pagan "religion." Individual man achieves it by acknowledging—that is, consciously willing—the existence of the idea, and by guiding his will with his reason or intellect.

In its most profound sense, this philosophy is not too different from the teaching of the Christian religion as interpreted by the Church. On the surface, however, it appeared contradictory to the then-contemporary doctrine of the Church that man is not himself free to direct his soul.

The scholars of Lorenzo the Magnificent's household, all of whom were fundamentally faithful to the Church, labored to find the harmony between the Platonic and the Christian points of view. They met informally to explain their latest conclusions and discuss them in sessions of what came to be known as the Platonic Academy—a cross between a learned society and a literary club—directed by Marsilio Ficino. These meetings generally took place in Lorenzo the Magnificent's beautiful country villas near Florence, where the tranquil, unworldly atmosphere seemed to reflect the character of Plato's world of ideas.

As a member of the Medici household, Michelangelo was, doubtless willingly, exposed to the cult of the Platonists with whom he continually associated. Thus there entered his mind, and firmly lodged there, a system of thought which would be in conflict with his conventional religious faith for at least fifty years.

As if this introduction to pagan philosophy were not perplexing enough to the mind of the adolescent Michelangelo, whose formal education had been brief, and conventional as well, in 1491 there appeared in Florence for the second time the fanatical Dominican monk, Girolamo Savonarola, who proceeded to deliver fiery sermons denouncing the paganism of the pleasure-loving city.

For not all of the diversions sponsored by Lorenzo the Magnificent were so serious as the symposiums of the Platonic Academy. The best known of Lorenzo's poems, which include several ribald Carnival songs, is the quatrain celebrating the pleasures of this world:

> Fair is youth and free of sorrow,
> Yet how soon its joys we bury!
> Let who would be now be merry;
> Sure is no one of tomorrow.

> —tr. Fletcher

Lorenzo diverted the attention of the Florentines from his political maneuvers, which were actually depriving them of certain of their liberties, by providing them with shows and festivals. Triumphs and processions, with floats and costumes and banners designed by accomplished artists including Francesco Granacci, and accompanied by hundreds of masked revelers on foot and on horseback, brightened the dark, twisting streets of Florence as they progressed by torchlight through the city until late at night. Lorenzo also revived the traditional May Day games in the Piazza Santa Trinità (Holy Trinity Square), which featured crowds of dancing girls singing the carefree songs that Poliziano composed for them. The learned men of Lorenzo's household were too progressive to be completely pious and reserved.

Michelangelo shared this side of their life also. He was fascinated by all poetry—the soul-searching cantos of Dante's *Commedia,* to which Cristoforo Landino, the great commentator on that poet and one of Lorenzo's circle, introduced him; the thunder of Poliziano's translation of Homer's *Iliad;* and the charming ballads that the handsome Luigi Pulci would improvise as he roamed the streets of Florence on a summer evening, and also recite in the Medici gatherings.

Michelangelo doubtless joined the other young folk of Florence on the steps of the cathedral, where, as a contemporary writer relates, they would "come and lay themselves full length during the season of extreme heat . . . because a fresh breeze is always blowing there, and the flags of white marble retain a certain coolness."

The same writer goes on to say of the Florentine youth: "They always have a thousand charming things to relate—as novels, intrigues, fables. They discuss duels, practical jokes, tricks played by men and women on each other—things witty, noble, decent, and in proper taste. I can swear that during all the hours I spent listening to their nightly dialogues, I never heard a word that was not comely and of good repute."

Savonarola was not so tolerant. Because Michelangelo's elder brother Lionardo was about to enter the Dominican Order, the Buonarroti family must have attended many of the fiery friar's terrifying sermons which sparked a religious revival in Florence. The message of doom that the monk's sepulchral voice boomed through the vaults of the Duomo appealed more to the poor and the reactionary than to the magnates of the city. Such de-nunciations of pleasure and luxury usually do. But Pico della Mirandola, who had induced Lorenzo the Magnificent to invite Savonarola back to Florence, said he felt cold shivers run through the marrow of his bones, and that his hairs stood on end as he listened to Savonarola. After another sermon, many Florentines were frightened into sobs and tears by Savonarola's picture of the horrors awaiting them, and went away through the streets without speaking, more dead than alive.

Savonarola had much to say about art. He cursed the blas-phemies he perceived in the work of such witty and worldly contemporary Florentine painters as Piero di Cosimo and Sandro Botticelli. Botticelli was converted from rendering pas-sages from Poliziano's poetry into such gorgeous evocations of the pagan spirit as *Primavera* and *The Birth of Venus* (in the Uffizi Gallery, Florence) or the *Venus and Mars* (in the National Gallery, London). Thereafter Botticelli painted only pensive Madonnas grieving over the sins of the world. Eventu-ally he stopped painting altogether.

For Savonarola maintained that all art should glorify God and His saints, and that only a painter whose life and thoughts were pure should be permitted to depict them. None but the most distinguished masters should paint in the churches, and they should paint only noble things, the friar announced. He enjoined painters not to use local models for their figures of holy personages so that the people would not be confused by the physical resemblance between a little-known saint and a well-known sinner. "Carnal and debauched men are the enemies of the fine arts," Savonarola declaimed; "every painter's works bear the stamp of his thoughts."

These fulminations are almost pure nonsense, and a more mature artist than Michelangelo or Botticelli would have seen them as such. In other respects, however, Savonarola came very close to the Platonists, especially when he spoke of beauty and of the perceptions of the artist. Probably this approximation on the friar's part of what the impressionable Michelangelo had heard in the Platonic Academy persuaded him that Savonarola was, as he later wrote to his monk-brother, "seraphic." As an old man, Michelangelo said that he could still hear Savonarola's thunder in his ears. Condivi reports that Savonarola and Dante were Michelangelo's greatest heroes.

The sixteen-year-old Michelangelo was clearly torn between the pull of Savonarola toward the religious faith he had learned from his family and the lure of the pagan past to freedom as expressed by the Platonists and in the antique statues that were forming his style. He knew that, in Savonarola's terms, he was already a sinner, possibly beyond redemption. The thought dismayed him that he might not be among the great and good who Savonarola said were alone worthy of practicing art. On the other hand, Michelangelo knew that his patron Lorenzo and the members of his circle were far from saintly, and it was these great men who encouraged his art.

This conflict in Michelangelo's mind is expressed in the two pieces of sculpture he executed in this period of uncoordinated moral values. These—one frankly pagan, and the other devoutly Christian—are the earliest of Michelangelo's genuine works in sculpture that survive. Both are now in the Casa Buonarroti, No. 70 Via Ghibellina, Florence, a museum dedi-

The Madonna of the Stairs (Casa Buonarroti, Florence)

cated to Michelangelo and located in the house he bought in 1508.

The Christian and earlier one is a small (22 x 16 inches) marble carved in very low relief with a heavily draped figure of the Virgin. In her lap is a nude infant Jesus, who snuggles against her breast, his head averted as if he were frightened by the four children playing on the steps at the base of which the Virgin sits. Hence the work is called *The Madonna of the Stairs*.

The Virgin gazes to the left, out of the roughhewn frame of the relief. There is no real psychological relationship between her and the Child, a design which suggests that the young Michelangelo is expressing his own separation from his mother. The major emphasis is on the Child—probably intended as a symbol of himself. All the lines direct the spectator's eyes to this infant. The spectator feels that he is looking directly at the Child, but looking up toward a remote Virgin.

The pagan piece, *Battle of the Centaurs*, was probably executed in late 1491 and early 1492. Michelangelo took the subject from the Roman poet Ovid's story (*Metamorphoses* XII) of Theseus' rescue of Hippodamia from the Centaurs who, as unruly guests at her wedding to Pirithous, king of the Lapiths, attempted to kidnap the bride. He used as a model a Roman sarcophagus which Bertoldo had also reinterpreted, but in bronze. Probably Michelangelo, always boldly competitive, wanted to show that he could equal, if not surpass, his teacher. Michelangelo's figures have better motivation for their actions than Bertoldo's, but the relief as a whole is inferior to the older sculptor's version of the subject.

Here, in much higher relief than the *Madonna of the Stairs*, are twenty-five figures in violent and complicated action. Yet the marble piece is still relatively small (34 x 36 inches).

Neither of these two sculptures is by any means a master-

Battle of the Centaurs (Casa Buonarroti, Florence)

piece, even though each shows an understanding of form and composition greater than what might be expected of so young an artist. Furthermore, the thinking expressed in the works is more mature than that of an ordinary adolescent.

In both pieces, however, Michelangelo is trying to say too much. They are overdetailed; one can hardly, as it were, see the woods for the trees. Michelangelo was not yet mature enough to understand that empty space can be as eloquent as filled space —that silence can be as evocative as speech. Nevertheless, he seems to have recognized that factor of communication. He works as if he sensed a conflict between the factor and the traditional obligation of contemporary artists to fill space with form, for the forms with which he filled his spaces are poorly executed. They are merely sketched, as if Michelangelo were reluctant to develop them completely. Moreover, their technique is faulty. The crude modeling suggests that Michelangelo did not consider the supplementary figures worthy of enough study to perfect them. Meaningless themselves, they confuse the meaning of the total work. It would be a long time before Michelangelo would learn to leave things out in order to achieve a simple, forceful expression of his intention.

What is remarkable about these two sculptures, especially the *Battle of the Centaurs,* is the impression Michelangelo gives the spectator that the figures are being liberated from the stone in which they had been existing as if in a prison. He implies that his task as an artist is to free them from this imprisonment. He seems to be creating form less than extracting form from formlessness. This approach, brand new in sculpture then, became Michelangelo's unique method. In the *Battle of the Centaurs* appears for the first time the contrast between mass and form, slavery and freedom, that was to give his sculpture the dynamic drive of life itself.

Michelangelo found great joy in creating these two works of sculpture. They were enthusiastically praised, and, considering the youth of the sculptor, justifiably so. They caused Michelangelo to recognize that from then on sculpture would be the most fertile field for his talents. He confessed that he resented the time he had devoted to learning to paint. Painting was not right for his nature. The few years he had spent with Ghirlandaio seemed to the boy irreplaceably wasted. For years afterward he seemed to be haunted by that loss of time.

Already aware of how time had speeded up as a result of the new extensions of man that the discoveries of the era had produced—the invention of printing and the revelation of a new world, to name the two most important—Michelangelo felt time to be a driving factor in his life. His own brief share of time, he feared, would soon be spent. He must make the most of what was left lest he perish leaving no mark behind. Of all the records of man's existence on this earth, none seemed to him more permanent than the antique sculptures that inspired him. Created long before him, they were still glorious, and would be long after he himself had vanished from the earthly scene. Sculpture alone would cause him to be remembered then.

Michelangelo left the *Battle of the Centaurs* rough. Few of his mature sculptures are smooth and highly polished in all their parts. They are the commissioned ones, not those he undertook to express an idea of his own. But this custom of Michelangelo's should not be taken to mean that he seldom completed a work. It means rather that he deliberately left a work "unfinished" in order to complete his communication— the drama of mass versus form.

Perhaps Michelangelo discovered by accident the effect of this contrast as a means of communication. He probably

stopped work on the *Battle of the Centaurs* because of the
death, on April 8, 1492, of his patron Lorenzo de' Medici, the
Magnificent. That event seemed to bring his world to an end.
Indeed, it brought to an end the greatness of Florence, though
Michelangelo could scarcely have foreseen that calamity.

III: FLIGHT AND FAME

After the simple funeral which the great Lorenzo had requested, Michelangelo left the sumptuous Medici palace for his father's modest house.

The death of his beloved patron at the early age of forty-three years not only grieved Michelangelo but filled him with foreboding. It was said that on his deathbed Lorenzo the Magnificent had first discoursed on Plato's doctrine of the soul's immortality. Then he had humbly called for Savonarola to grant him absolution. The friar, who up to then had narrowmindedly snubbed Lorenzo as impious, came to the dying man's bedside, but refused to give his blessing.

The influence of Savonarola, the reactionary reformer, became greater than ever, both with the anti-Medici party and with the Mediceans. For Lorenzo's deathbed call for the friar seemed to the Medici supporters a recognition by their departed leader of Savonarola's prestige.

The unprivileged people of Florence were on Savonarola's side anyway, because he had pleaded their cause against the capricious system of taxation Lorenzo had induced the signoria to adopt. Savonarola had also taken a stand against Lorenzo's use of public funds for his own purposes. The death of Pope Innocent VIII occurred three and a half months after Lorenzo the Magnificent's, and since Savonarola had foretold that, the monk was now regarded as a prophet.

In the devout Buonarroti household there was no doubt that Savonarola was as much a voice of God as the Old Testament prophets whose stern demands for repentance the friar was interpreting in his sermons. Deprived of the antidote to Savonarola provided by the calm discourses of the Platonic Academy, Michelangelo became convinced that he himself was being denounced by the friar. Could he ever be virtuous enough to become the type of artist Savonarola insisted should be the only one to work for God?

For a long time Michelangelo's confusion of mind, dejection, and despair kept him from working. Probably at this time he pored over the Bible and over Dante's perplexing poem on the journey of the soul in an effort to find some solution of his private problem, some hope for himself as a human being. The Platonist scholars had advised against studying the Bible because its imperfect Latin might corrupt the reader's style.

Certainly, Michelangelo, early in his career, had as complete a knowledge of the Bible and of Dante's *Commedia* as any scholar. From his deep study of both, as from his study of antique sculpture, he derived new and uniquely personal interpretations. Other scholars had to admit that these were logical and defensible. Upon both expressions of spiritual comfort—the Bible and the *Commedia*—Michelangelo stamped his own self-expression.

For an ill-educated man, Michelangelo did a vast amount of reading throughout his life. He was familiar with the works of the ancients—Homer, Sappho, Vergil, Ovid, Plato, Pliny, Plotinus, Pythagoras, Lucretius, and Plutarch—as well as later authors. He always kept up with the major literary men of his time. He also knew the works of writers, both ancient and contemporary, on art and architecture. Traces of these authors, references to them, and sometimes long paraphrases from them occur in his poems and letters. Their ideas are frequently reflected in his paintings and sculpture.

Michelangelo's harmonization of the Christian and pagan attitudes for the time being was his conclusion that through man's body, the human intellect is connected to and incited by all physical things. The nude human body, so worshiped by ancient artists, therefore appeared to Michelangelo as the supreme manifestation of God in the world, the noblest of His creations, the most like Himself. In one of his sonnets Michelangelo later wrote of the nude male body:

Nor does God in his grace show himself to me elsewhere
More clearly than in a graceful and mortal veil.
And that alone I love because in this He is mirrored.
                                        —tr. Clements

Michelangelo found that the difference between the artist Savonarola described and an incompetent one lies in the degree to which the artist's intellect is sensitive to beauty. The artist must use his intellect to find what has not been found before. The intellect is, therefore, a discovering power. For art forms exist whether artists exist or not, as God exists whether or not man can find Him.

These conceptions, derived from the pagan Plato, led Michelangelo to the Christian conclusion that it was his duty first to find God in His work. Then he must reveal God to others by his own work.

The sense of duty, however, seldom brings with it the ability to fulfill the obligation. Instead, that sense usually produces in a conscientious individual an agonizing tension between his desire and its accomplishment. Such a tension began to plague Michelangelo until his feelings writhed as his body might twist

and turn under physical torture. The intensity of that unre-
solved tension caused Michelangelo to see all human life as
similarly tortured. He needed subjects to express this attitude.
Only thus could they release his own tensions.

Michelangelo then reached the conclusion that his subjects
could be either Christian or pagan. The subject would be
merely his medium of communication of the nature of God.
God, he recognized, created both Christian and pagan men.
Both were, as God Himself said, His image and likeness.

Michelangelo resolved, therefore, that he must study man.
By understanding man and the idealistic man's constant striving to regain the identity with God that man lost through the
first man's disobedience, Michelangelo felt that he might not
only understand God, but also rescue himself from the spiritual
torture he was experiencing.

Hence Michelangelo undertook to learn human anatomy by
dissecting corpses. The progressive prior of Santo Spirito (Holy
Ghost) Monastery, Niccolò Bichiellini, provided him with
cadavers from the monastery's hospital, and gave him a room in
which to work—at night by the light of a candle, and secretly,
for such dissections were only barely legal.

The grisly work and the stench of the unembalmed bodies
sickened Michelangelo, but he kept at it until he had mastered
the marvelous secrets of human musculature and the articula-
tion of the bones. Hence he learned the mechanism behind
every one of the innumerable movements of which the human
body is capable, something few other artists grasped then or, for
that matter, understand even now.

Out of gratitude to the prior of Santo Spirito, Michelangelo
carved a crucifix from poplar wood for the monastery. This
work was lost for a long time. When it was rediscovered in
1962, most authorities accepted it as a genuine product of

The *Crucifix for Santo Spirito* (Casa Buonarroti, Florence)

Michelangelo's hands. It is now in the Casa Buonarroti in Florence.

This crucifix, a little smaller than life-size, shows how clear Michelangelo's thinking on the relationship of paganism and Christianity had become. The nude boyish body—a pagan form—of the Christ suggests the Platonic innocence and purity of the soul. The adult face suggests Christ's mature renunciation of bitterness at his persecution, and his resignation to the will of God. The body is twisted in the serpentine form that would be a dominant characteristic of Michelangelo's figures. The torsion expresses Michelangelo's own writhing spirit. The swirl of the body—man and God in one—directs the spectator's eyes upward to the sensitively modeled face with its compassionate expression. The musculature shows how precisely Michelangelo was applying his new knowledge of "divine" human anatomy.

At approximately the same time, 1492, Michelangelo was working on a pagan subject. He had bought an abandoned block of marble, and was extracting from it a *Hercules* eight feet in height. This subject also expressed his spiritual conclusions. Hercules, the semidivine Greek hero, had to accomplish twelve tasks of superhuman difficulty before he could be admitted into the pagan conception of Heaven. Hercules, moreover, was of prodigious size and strength—a believable image of God's immensity and power.

That gigantic *Hercules* disappeared in 1714. Drawings made of it by other artists indicate only that it was a standing nude figure, strong and slender.

A heavy snowfall on January 20, 1494, brought Michelangelo back into the Medici household. Piero de' Medici, the eldest son of Lorenzo the Magnificent, had succeeded his father as head of the family and as the unofficial ruler of democratic Florence.

Piero was vastly different from Lorenzo the Magnificent. He was insufferably proud and tactless, and none too intelligent. A proficient athlete himself, his interest was in sports. Hence the snowfall suggested to him a snowball fight in the courtyard of his palace, and he sent for Michelangelo to fashion a gigantic snowman as a decoration for the frolic. Michelangelo recognized the insult to himself as a sculptor who believed his works would be a permanent record of his stay on earth, but he accepted the commission.

Thereafter, Piero invited Michelangelo to live again in the Medici palace, but Michelangelo declined. Life, he knew, would be so different in that household under the arrogant Piero that he would be constantly and sadly reminded of the golden days of Lorenzo the Magnificent. Besides, Michelangelo had found a new and independent life for himself, and was engrossed in work on his *Hercules*. But he did occasionally go back to his old room in the palace, probably for some festivity or other, and Piero always praised his abilities. To Piero's insensitive mind they were on an equal level with the athletic prowess of his handsome Spanish groom who could run as fast as a galloping horse.

Michelangelo's coolness toward Piero de' Medici was due less to Piero's tactless comparisons than to the influence of Savonarola upon the artist's thinking. Savonarola had been hostile to Lorenzo the Magnificent on principle; he was hostile to Piero both on principle and on the basis of the man's personality. In the two years following Lorenzo's death, Piero's irresponsible conduct greatly strengthened Savonarola's influence on the people of Florence. They looked to the friar for moral guidance in the perilous times that were approaching.

For, on August 22, 1494, the half-crazy King Charles VIII of France led his terrifying army into northern Italy to assert his feudal rights to the Kingdom of Naples. Piero de' Medici rashly declared Florence an ally of that southern Italian realm, thus trapping Florence between the two foes. Piero could easily have annihilated the French army as it was negotiating the narrow Florentine territory between the mountains and the sea. Instead, he cravenly surrendered the Tuscan fortresses to the invaders and promised them an enormous tribute.

The Florentines were furious over this capitulation. Before Piero returned to the city from the French camp, where he had sold out to King Charles, it was clear that there would be an uprising against the treachery of the Medici.

As an intimate of the hapless Piero, Michelangelo recognized that a rebellion against the Medici would undoubtedly not spare their friends and partisans. Since Michelangelo's loyalty to Piero was hardly strong, and since he had no wish to have his promising career interrupted and perhaps terminated by a vengeful mob, Michelangelo took off with two companions from seething Florence. They crossed the Apennine mountains to independent Bologna, some fifty miles to the northeast. From there they proceeded to Venice.

In Venice they learned that on November 9, the signoria had expelled Piero de' Medici from Florence, and that the enraged Florentines had sacked the Medici palace, the sculpture garden, and the houses of several Medici adherents. Piero and his brother, Cardinal Giovanni, fled by the same route that Michelangelo had taken, and likewise arrived in Venice. The signoria offered a generous reward for their return, either alive or dead.

Michelangelo could easily see that Venice was too small for both him and these wanted persons. There was good reason for him to believe that anyone after the reward might well include him as a Medici partisan in the bloody booty. He and his traveling companions decided to go back to progressive Bologna, whose intellectual atmosphere was like that of Florence. Michelangelo had already found that in Bologna he had a reputation as an artist of distinction, whereas the Venetians had rather ignored his talents.

As a precaution in these times of war, with the fearsome French army likely to appear before the gates of Bologna at any time, the ruler of the city, Giovanni Bentivogli, had made entrance into its gates conditional upon a traveler giving the password. Presumably only a loyal Bolognese would know this. When Michelangelo and his companions, who had neglected to learn the password during their previous visit, were unable to clear themselves, they were thrown into jail as suspicious characters, and fined. They could not pay the fine.

Giovanfrancesco Aldovrandi, a member of the Bolognese city council, happened to visit the prison. Michelangelo procured an interview with this nobleman, and so impressed him with his doleful story that Aldovrandi got the young artist released and offered him hospitality. Michelangelo gave his friends all the money he had with him so that they could pay their fine, and went home with Aldovrandi.

Bologna's Church of San Domenico (St. Dominic) contained the tomb of the founder of the great Order of Preachers, who had died in the city in 1221. The lavish shrine above it had been begun in 1270, but was still unfinished. Admiring the sculptures on the shrine, Michelangelo convinced his host that he could continue the artistic tradition. Aldovrandi bought him the marble for the statues needed to complete the shrine and paid him for his work as a donation to the church from the Aldovrandi family.

The most interesting of the two-foot-high figures Michelangelo carved is that of the soldier-martyr St. Proculus. Michelangelo endowed this statuette with a sense of vigorous

St. Proculus (St. Dominic, Bologna)

movement, and planted a fierce expression on the face. The saint is a soldier of the Lord fighting valiantly against evil. Michelangelo had obviously studied Verocchio's bronze *General Bartolommeo Colleoni* in Venice, and he carried much of the force of that huge equestrian masterpiece over into the little figure of St. Proculus.

Michelangelo's statue of St. Petronius, a bishop, is calmer and more majestic, and the face is spiritual. The long, flowing robes give it a dignity lacking in the tight-fitting Bolognese costume of St. Proculus. The pair make a neat statement about life and time—the sturdy, aggressive youth, and the serene old man.

Michelangelo's little (twenty inches high) angel with a candlestick balances one by the previous sculptor who worked on the tomb of St. Dominic, Niccolò dell' Arca. That one is refined and pensive, feminine and soft to the point of sentimentality. Michelangelo's angel is masculine, and far more dynamic in organization and execution. The pair dramatically demonstrates Michelangelo's superiority over his predecessors.

There was still one more figure to be made for the shrine, but a local sculptor belligerently asserted to the city government his right to complete the tomb over that of Michelangelo, a foreigner. Consequently Michelangelo left Bologna abruptly, and with regret at having to desert his benefactor, Giovanfrancesco Aldovrandi. He had earned his board and keep at Aldovrandi's house by reading aloud to his host the works of the Tuscan poets. Aldovrandi loved to hear the poems of Dante and Petrarch rendered in their native accent, which Michelangelo never abandoned.

Again time was hounding Michelangelo. He felt that he had been wasting time on work within such small dimensions as the figures on the tomb of St. Dominic. There his statues would be somewhat lost among figures by lesser sculptors; they would not

St. Petronius (St. Dominic, Bologna)

Angel with Candlestick (St. Dominic, Bologna)

stand alone to proclaim his own intellect and his vision. He was eager to get back to the gigantic *Hercules* he had left unfinished in Florence.

By the time he reached Florence, at the end of 1495, there was a new government in the city. The organization and the democratic principles of this regime were largely due to Savonarola. Its emphasis on the freedom of the individual and on his right to participate in the direction of his city-state appealed to Michelangelo.

The Florentines welcomed Michelangelo as an anti-Medicean after his year of exile. He immediately got a commission from one of the leaders of the new democratic government —Lorenzo di Pierfrancesco de' Medici, of the younger branch of the Medici family, who had been prominent in the rebellion that exiled his cousins in 1494.

For this patron Michelangelo executed a marble *Young St. John the Baptist*, the favorite saint of the Florentines. All trace of this statue has been lost, and nothing is now known of it.

The pagan side of Michelangelo's thinking was still strong, roused perhaps by the sober, penitential atmosphere of Florence under Savonarola's heavy influence. For much as Michelangelo was swayed by the reforming friar, he kept his own independence of mind. He could not forget his glimpses of the Platonic world with its theme of self-determination. Hence, Michelangelo followed the Christian *St. John* with a pagan *Sleeping Cupid*—or, perhaps, worked simultaneously on the two statues.

That life-size marble, which was a noncommissioned work, disappeared in a London fire in 1698. Considerably more is known about it, however, than about the *St. John*. A dealer, Baldassare del Milanesi, bought it for thirty ducats, buried it in earth so as to make it appear an antique, and sold it to Raffaello Riario, Cardinal di San Giorgio, in Rome, for two hundred ducats. Cardinal Riario, however, discovered the trick, and sent the *Cupid* back to the dishonest dealer.

The cardinal also sent an agent to find the sculptor, who he had learned was in Florence. Michelangelo naïvely admitted to this agent that the *Cupid* was indeed his work. Angry at having been defrauded of 170 ducats, Michelangelo determined to go to Rome in order either to collect that sum from Baldassare Milanesi or get the statue back.

The agent persuaded Michelangelo that Cardinal Riario was more eager to have the talented young sculptor in his service than he was angry at having been deceived about the antiquity of the *Cupid*. He also persuaded Michelangelo that Rome would offer him much wider recognition than could Florence.

At least partially convinced, Michelangelo took the precaution of getting from Lorenzo di Pierfrancesco de' Medici letters of introduction to important persons in Rome, and also a letter of credit to a Florentine banker there. He wanted no repetition of the Bologna incident. Fortified with these, Michelangelo set out on the three-day journey to Rome, and on Saturday, June 24, 1496, presented himself and his letter of introduction to the white-faced Cardinal Riario at his new, immense, and gorgeous palace, now the Palazzo della Cancellaria, on the Corso Vittorio Emanuele.

The agent put Michelangelo up in his house near that palace. On the following day, Sunday, June 25, Cardinal Riario invited Michelangelo to see his collection of antique sculptures. After Michelangelo had praised their beauty, the cardinal asked him whether he had the courage to attempt an equally beautiful sculpture. Michelangelo accepted the challenge. The cardinal bought him a block of marble for a life-size figure, and on Monday, July 3, Michelangelo began work on it—but what it was is now unknown.

So far as is known, Michelangelo did not complete any work

for Cardinal Riario, but the cardinal apparently provided him
with money during his stay in Rome, for Michelangelo wrote
his father about buying blocks of marble, and he could afford to
give his brother Lionardo enough money to get home from a
visit to him. But Michelangelo also wrote that in matters of
money he had to "go slowly" with such "grand masters, because
they cannot be coerced." He was finding life in Rome considerably more complicated than it was in provincial Florence.

Michelangelo also got work from some of the many rich
Florentine merchants and bankers who were doing business in
Rome. Piero de' Medici, who had drifted to Rome to enjoy the
protection of his brother, Cardinal Giovanni, commissioned a
statue. In the summer of 1497, Michelangelo bought the
marble for it, but Piero, who was living a riotous life as the head
of the exiled branch of the Medici family, reneged on the
agreement.

Michelangelo found a more reliable patron in Jacopo Gallo, a
Roman banker to whom he was introduced by a friend of the
Buonarroti family. Gallo bought a life-size standing nude—
probably the one that Michelangelo had begun for Piero de'
Medici. This was another *Cupid* or an *Apollo*; it, too, has
disappeared. Gallo also commissioned a *Bacchus* from Michelangelo.

A more important commission came to Michelangelo in 1497
from the French Abbot of St. Denis, Jean de Villiers de la
Groslaye, who had just been made a cardinal and therefore
wanted to leave a memorial of himself in Rome. He ordered a
Pietà—that is, a group representing the Virgin holding the
dead Christ—and Michelangelo made plans and sketches for it
in the summer of 1497. By November of that year he had gone
to the marble quarries of Carrara to select the stone for this
group. It took him over three months to find a block large and
beautiful enough, and also one in which he could see impris-

oned his concept of the figures he would liberate from the living stone.

It was the first of many expeditions Michelangelo made to the Carrara mountains near the Ligurian coast. He seemed to find their hoard of "alpine rock," as he called it, a source of strength. Later he would see giants embedded in their crags, colossi beseeching him to release them. There God, the master sculptor, had planted Michelangelo's destiny. He began to dream of carving an entire mountain into the form he saw embedded in it. The vision haunted him throughout his lifetime. The mountains of Carrara seemed the only thing in nature grand enough to match his expanding intellect.

The contract for the *Pietà* was not signed until August 27, 1498. Doubtless all parties had been waiting for the safe arrival in Rome of the marble Michelangelo had selected; the piece would have had to be cut by some trusted representative of his, and then shipped. Jacopo Gallo witnessed the document, and added to it a pledge that the sculpture "shall be the finest work in marble which Rome today can show, and that no master of our days shall be able to produce a better."

In the months between March and August, 1498, Michelangelo had begun his *Bacchus* for Gallo. For the next two years he worked simultaneously on both that and the *Pietà*—the pagan god and the Christian one. Could Michelangelo have sensed what, centuries later, anthropologists were to demonstrate about the fundamental similarity between these two superficially opposite expressions of the mysteries of life, resurrection, and immortality?

Probably the *Bacchus,* now in the Bargello in Florence, was completed first. The nude figure of the god is nearly six feet seven inches in height. It is supported—and adorned by—a mischievously grinning faun who perches on a tree stump while nibbling at a bunch of grapes. With his right foot the god is

Bacchus (Bargello, Florence)

beating out the measure of the dance with which his unseen
worshipers are reverencing him. In his right hand he holds a
wine cup—none too steadily, it seems, for his expression and
the relaxed pose of his youthful body show that he is drunk on
the wine of life that is his symbol. His head is crowned with the
fruit and the leaves of the vines he protects as life-givers; from
his lax left hand dangles an animal's skin—probably intended
to be that of a panther, the lithe beast that is Bacchus' attribute,
but which Michelangelo had doubtless never seen alive. The
voluptuously modeled body is almost feminine from the front
view, but vigorously muscled in the rear. The whole tone of
the god is sleepy and supple and trancelike, as if he were
overcome by his own intoxicating power. In humorous contrast,
the little faun is wigglingly alert.

Vastly different is the *Pietà*, which was probably not finished
until 1500, after the death of Cardinal de la Groslaye. It is now
in the Chapel of the Pietà, just to the right of the entrance to
St. Peter's Church in Rome. Here it is placed rather too high; it
was designed to be seen at eye level. It is probably the best
known and most beloved statue of the Western world. It is also
one of the most nearly perfect—an astonishing achievement for
any sculptor, even more extraordinary for a twenty-five-year-old
one.

The pyramidal group is only 68.5 inches high and 68.6
inches wide at the base. Like the *Bacchus*, it is of highly
polished marble. The young Virgin-mother sits on a rock, holding the limp figure of her dead Son on her lap. Her right hand
under his right arm supports his chest; her left hand is extended
in a lyrical gesture of resignation. Serene resignation to the will
of God is indeed the principal characteristic of this girl who
seems to have known that this moment of sacrifice had been
ordained since the beginning of time. Her lap seems an altar on
which the sacrifice has been performed. Human love for the

Pietà or *Madonna della Febbre* (St. Peter's, Rome)

Son, human agony over His painful physical end, and all sense of loss have been absorbed into mystical wonder at the way God's will has been effected.

The Christ is also a youthful figure. It is relaxed, as the *Bacchus* is, but in a slumber from which He soon shall wake. Death here is but a temporary phase of existence. The body is delicately modeled to emphasize the spiritual quality of the man on whom the humiliating scars of physical punishment have already almost vanished. All around swirl the folds of the Virgin's robe as if they were time enfolding the endless cycle of life and death evolving one from the other. For at the very moment depicted in the statue one great age has ended and another has begun.

On the band across the Virgin's breast, Michelangelo later carved in Roman letters: *Michelāgelus Bonarotus Florent. Faciebat* ("Michelangelo Buonarroti, the Florentine, made this"). He did this after he had heard some Lombard spectators expressing their disbelief that so young a man as Michelangelo could have created so mature a masterpiece. They attributed it to their countryman, Christoforo Solari of Milan ("Il Gobbo"). No other sculpture or painting by Michelangelo bears his name.

Michelangelo justified his representation of the Virgin as younger in appearance than her Son by saying that since she was a paragon of chastity, her youth would have been preserved, perhaps to convince the world of her unsullied purity.

That theological argument, worthy of the minute analyses of a medieval scholastic philosopher, and an example of what today might be called "pious piffle," greatly impressed some of Michelangelo's contemporaries. Probably Michelangelo invented it on the spur of a moment as an answer to some pedantic criticism, and did not intend it to be taken seriously. It shows, however, how much medieval thinking still existed in an age that is sometimes thought to have totally discarded the philosophy of the previous era. The group itself shows how much Michelangelo's thinking about the subject differed from that of the Middle Ages. Then a *pietà* was a scene of hysterical grief and lamentation. Here the terrible tension of grief is implied rather than stated. Michelangelo saw in the scene only mystical contemplation—timeless, hence ageless.

The *Pietà*, sometimes called the "Madonna della Febbre" (Madonna of the Fever) because it was first placed in the chapel of that name, brought Michelangelo the recognition he had come to Rome to seek.

IV: HONOR AT HOME

Recognition was a private joy to Michelangelo, no reason for public display. Letters between him and his family in Florence indicate that he had little money to spare and that he had no lodging of his own but boarded with some Roman family or other. When his favorite brother, Buonarroto, visited him after the death of their stepmother in July, 1497, Michelangelo had to put him up at an inn—treatment for which Michelangelo feebly apologized, for inns at that time were filthy and unsafe. But Michelangelo had a studio of his own and employed at least one *garzone*—a combination of manservant, helper, and apprentice.

After a second visit in 1500, Buonarroto reported to their father that Michelangelo lived with great economy. Lodovico Buonarroti advised Michelangelo not to be so stingy as to endanger his health and his disposition. He also advised his second son to be sure to keep his head warm and never to wash, but to get a rubdown instead. Not washing may have been a custom in Florence—Lorenzo the Magnificent had no sense of smell—but Romans prided themselves on their cleanliness and frequently went swimming in the Tiber.

However penny-pinching Michelangelo may have been in respect to his own wants and needs, he was generous to his family. Their financial situation worried him; he would continue to be concerned about them for the rest of his life. Lodovico still kept his job in the customs office in Florence, but he was a weak and foolish man, more or less continually in debt. Michelangelo's two youngest brothers were stupid and worthless. Buonarroto, for whom Michelangelo bought a small wool business, was at least responsible, but hardly a person of any distinction.

With a population of only eighty-five thousand, Rome was a slightly smaller city than Florence. Having no industries, Rome lacked the competitive spirit of other cities, especially Florence. Hence it created few artists of its own; it imported them, as Michelangelo had been imported, to work for the fabulously rich churchmen who made up the top stratum of Roman society.

These cardinals and bishops got their wealth from the revenues of their benefices—lands, cities, and villages that the Church had acquired over the centuries. The pope awarded benefices to the prelates for political reasons. Piety was no criterion for high office in the Church; few of its princes practiced it in either their private or public lives. They were, in effect, feudal lords. Rome, therefore, was still medieval in tone. The atmosphere of the city had little if any of the progressive spirit of free enterprise that made Florence vivid and vital.

Rome was also a turbulent city. The bitter feud between the Orsini and the Colonna families, which had been going on for about two hundred years, still would break out from time to time. The fearful rivalry between Pope Alexander VI and Cardinal Giuliano della Rovere (later Pope Julius II) also produced considerable violence. There were, on the average, nine murders committed every day. No prudent person, even remotely associated with one or another of these warring factions, left the comparative safety of his house without putting on a shirt of light chain mail under his outer garments and equipping himself with at least a dagger for protection. Michelangelo, who was something of a physical coward, had no wish to attract an assassin by joining the household of a powerful Roman or by competing for a commission from the pope or one of his many enemies.

The splendor of Rome, which at that time appeared mostly in the gorgeous palaces of the nobles, seems to have left Michelangelo unmoved. He never mentioned that aspect of the Eternal City in his letters home; they are almost wholly devoted to personal matters. Most of the glorious remains of ancient Rome were still half-buried under the debris of a thousand years. Few of the great statues of antiquity had yet been found, though the ruins were being excavated for the sake of building stones for the construction of palaces and churches. The *Apollo Belvedere*, for example, was not discovered until 1503; the *Laocoön*, not until 1506.

Still a simple, introspective young man, Michelangelo was homesick for Florence. Florence had recovered from the hectic Savonarola episode. That had ended on May 23, 1498, with the execution of the half-mad friar. Another constitution was in the process of construction; it would subordinate the inefficient signoria, which changed composition every two months, to an executive elected for life as a kind of permanent dictator. The man most likely to procure that executive office of gonfalonier (minister of justice or chief magistrate) was Piero Soderini, a well-intentioned and generally respected person, but one of mediocre ability. Soderini was an old friend of the Buonarroti family, hence likely to employ for state commissions the young sculptor whose fame had reached his hometown. Therefore, when Michelangelo's friends in Florence kept urging him to return to that city, he was delighted to do so.

Michelangelo arrived in Florence before the new constitu-

tion was officially adopted; hence, the commission he expected
from the government could not be granted. In the meantime he
signed a contract with Cardinal Francesco Piccolomini of Siena
to create within three years fifteen statues of male saints for the
altar of the Piccolomini Chapel in the Cathedral of Siena. By
the time the three years were up, Michelangelo had completed
only four of these: St. Peter and St. Paul, and possibly St.
Gregory and St. Pius. (The latter two may have been designed
by Michelangelo, but were probably executed by assistants.)
They seem to have been done hastily and without enthusiasm.
The only interesting aspect of these uninspired works is that
they show the influence of Donatello's sculpture on Michelangelo. He was at a critical time in his career, passing from his
experimental phase into his first mature one.

On August 16, 1501, twelve days after the new constitution
had been adopted, Michelangelo received the commission from
the Florentine Republic for which he had been waiting. In his
contract with Cardinal Piccolomini, Michelangelo had agreed
not to accept any other commissions until the statues for Siena
were done, but he could not resist this one from the signoria,
which Soderini had thrown his way. To renege on the Piccolomini contract troubled Michelangelo's conscience. Nevertheless, he was haunted by the thought that he might be wasting
his time on such minor work, and he was flattered by being
offered a commission that the great Leonardo da Vinci had
turned down. Consequently, Michelangelo signed the signoria's contract stipulating delivery of a colossal *David* within
two years.

The seventeen-foot piece of marble placed at Michelangelo's
disposal for this statue belonged to the *operai* (construction
department) of Florence's cathedral. The operai had purchased
it in 1464 for a sculptor who damaged it in blocking out his
"giant or Hercules" and so was released from his contract. At

St. Peter (Cathedral, Siena)

St. Paul (Cathedral, Siena)

least one other sculptor had tried to make something out of the
enormous and valuable piece of marble, but it lay undeveloped
until the late spring of 1501, when another sculptor demanded
it as a gift. Before the operai granted this request, they sent for
Michelangelo to inspect the marble and advise them what to do
about it. On or about July 2, 1501, Michelangelo convinced
them that he could fashion a *David* from the damaged block
without adding other pieces—something Florentine sculptors
were loath to do, although other sculptors frequently did.

On September 9, three weeks after the contract was signed,
Michelangelo began testing the marble for hardness. He had
probably spent the intervening time in making preparatory
sketches and perhaps a wax model for his statue. "On September 13, a Monday, very early in the morning, he began work on
the block firmly and bravely"—so says a marginal note on the
contract. By October 13, he had made a wooden shed around
the block so that he could work under cover throughout the
winter. By February 28, 1502, the statue was half-finished, and
by January 25, 1504, near enough to completion for the appointment of a committee to choose a site for it.

The committee included such master artists as Leonardo da
Vinci, Sandro Botticelli, Pietro Perugino, Lorenzo di Credi,
and Piero di Cosimo. Another member was Michelangelo's
boyhood friend, Francesco Granacci. Probably at no other time
in history were so many artists of the first rank joined in one
endeavor or working simultaneously in one city.

The committee voted to place the work in the graceful
Loggia (pavilion) opposite the palace of the signoria (now
known, respectively, as the Loggia dei Lanzi for the lancers who
were later quartered in it, and as the Palazzo Vecchio, or Old
Palace). The cathedral officials, however, overruled this major-
ity opinion, and decided to set the statue beside the doorway to

the palace of the signoria, on the axis of the tower, where Donatello's *Judith* then stood.

That fine statue was moved a little to the east, where it now stands. It once served to represent Florence's delivery from its enemies (see the apocryphal *Book of Judith*), but that symbolism had become meaningless. The *Judith* was even thought to be a bad omen. David, the protector of the liberties of the Hebrews, was now seen as a more fitting guardian for the building where the Florentine government met to maintain the liberty of the city.

The next problem was moving the gigantic statue from Michelangelo's shed near the cathedral to the palace of the signoria, about a quarter-mile distant. The architect brothers Antonio and Giuliano Sangallo, with the help of other engineers and of Michelangelo himself, constructed an enclosure over fourteen rollers. In the middle of this framework the statue was hung, so that it could sway freely as the vehicle jolted.

On May 14, 1504, over forty men began turning the windlass that moved the crate. The trip took four days. On June 8, the *David* was finally set on the platform where the *Judith* had been. A new base was finished for it on September 8. (In 1873, the *David* was removed to the shelter of the hall of the Academy of Fine Arts on the Piazza San Marco; a copy now stands by the door of the Palazzo Vecchio.)

The thirteen-and-a-half-foot-high nude figure represents the Hebrew hero as a stalwart adolescent preparing to slay the Philistine giant Goliath (I Samuel 17:32–54). Previous renditions of the story showed a boyish David after he has killed Goliath, and with the giant's head in his hand or at his feet. Michelangelo asserted his independence and the freshness of his vision by conceiving David as he resolutely takes up the challenge and plans his strategy. The whole majestic pose of the superbly modeled athletic body, and the expression of the

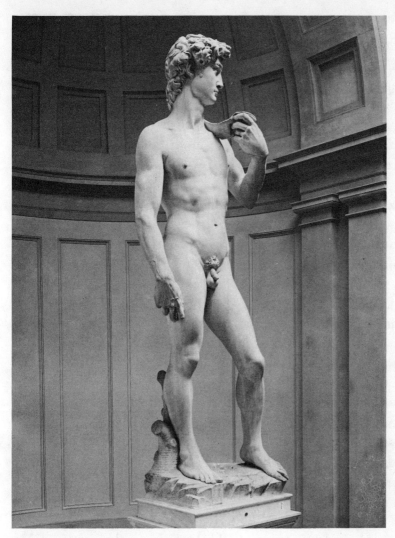

David (Academy of Fine Arts, Florence)

face, are so charged with forceful determination that they have an awe-inspiring effect on the spectator. Here, for the first time, appears the *terribilità* that characterizes most of Michelangelo's mature work—a quality of powerful thought and emotion expressed in a human body so vigorously that the figure becomes more than human, more than alive. Hence it is terrifying to contemplate what it would be like if indeed it were alive.

The Florentines gazed at their splendid new monument with feelings that must have been like these. At any rate, they admired, they wondered, and they praised. No criticism was heard except that of Piero Soderini, who thought the *David*'s nose too long.

Michelangelo hid some marble dust in one hand, took chisel and mallet in the other, and climbed up to remedy this "defect" and please his new patron. Once on a level with the nose of the *gigante*—for so the Florentines immediately nicknamed the statue—he pretended to carve a bit, and let the marble dust fall before Soderini without changing a thing.

"Ah," said the amiable but unperceptive gonfalonier, "that is much better. Now you have really brought it to life."

Leonardo da Vinci's criticism was silently to make a sketch of the *David* with the gap between the legs closed, thus concentrating the volume. True enough, the stance of the *David* is antiquated and a little awkward. Michelangelo may have been forced into this design by the damage that the original block of marble had suffered. More likely, however, he considered the pose typical of an adolescent tensed for attack, just as the oversize hands are typical of a youth not yet maturely proportioned.

The tension of the figure, emphasized by the torsion of the left leg and by the sharply bent wrists, contrasts with the restraint expressed by the steady position of the head and the steadfast gaze of the eyes. A moment of time has been captured forever. In another moment, the sling will be snapped over the shoulder, the deadly stone will fly, and the power implicit in the body will contort it into violent action. Like all great art, therefore, the *David* is not a static being but is in a state of becoming—not "true to life," but truer than life.

Michelangelo's rivalry with the twenty-three-years-older Leonardo da Vinci was more aggressive than the maturer artist's patiently silent rebuke to the impetuous young sculptor, whom he doubtless regarded as something of a puppy. Leonardo had deserted Florence for Milan in 1482, but had returned to his native city in 1499 as a refugee from the French armies which had driven his Milanese patron, Duke Lodovico Sforza, into exile. The Florentines, who had long beseeched the phenomenal Leonardo to come back to them, regarded him as the greatest genius of Florentine history, if not of all time—a fairly accurate judgment. This adulation nettled Michelangelo, who, still as sharp-tongued as when he had provoked Torrigiano to hit him, had publicly taunted Leonardo about an equestrian statue he had failed to finish. Michelangelo rudely implied that Leonardo lacked the skill to complete it, whereas the truth was that politics prevented Leonardo from casting the statue in bronze.

Part of Michelangelo's antagonism to Leonardo da Vinci must have been due to his private acknowledgment that at that time Leonardo had forgotten more than Michelangelo knew. In 1501, Leonardo exhibited in Florence a cartoon for his *Madonna and Child with St. Anne,* now in the Louvre, Paris. Michelangelo seems to have meditated deeply on this drawing, in which the Virgin reaches for her infant Son as she sits on the lap of her mother. The mystical quality of the painting of the subject, which Leonardo completed in Florence in 1502 or 1503, also greatly impressed Michelangelo.

Leonardo da Vinci's influence appears strong in the first independent painting that survives from Michelango's hand.

It was commissioned by a Florentine wool merchant, Angelo Doni, as a wedding present for Maddalena Strozzi, whom he married early in 1504. Hence the painting is known as the *Doni Holy Family* and was probably done in late 1503 or early 1504. It is now in Florence's Uffizi Gallery.

In shape the work, which is painted on wood, is a *tondo* (circle) 47.25 inches in diameter. It is enclosed in a wide, heavily sculptured frame which is an integral part of the work and was designed by Michelangelo himself. The circular shape demands a precise balance of the pictorial elements, and one of the most remarkable aspects of the work is the balance that Michelangelo achieved with the monumental figures he arranged in a startlingly unconventional design.

The composition of the principal group—the Virgin, the infant Jesus, and St. Joseph—is clearly derived from Leonardo. The Virgin turns from the book she has been reading to lift down over her shoulder the child whom St. Joseph, seated behind her, is handing to her. Her body twists in the serpentine line that was becoming a dominant characteristic of Michelangelo's design—an expression of his spiritual anguish.

Behind this central group an impish little St. John peers at them over a semicircular gray coping. He is like the pagan faun in the *Bacchus*. Beyond is a semicircular wall against which loll five nude male figures. In the far distance is a dim coastal landscape.

This landscape, and the clumps of grass and clover around the seated Virgin, are the only touches of nature in the work. Michelangelo disliked employing items in nature as decoration; he thought contemporary Flemish painters' detailed trees, flowers, mountains, and rocks distracting. Instead, he used for decoration in the *Doni Holy Family* the five male nudes, thus emphasizing his conviction that the human form is the only true artistic symbol.

The *Doni Madonna* (Uffizi, Florence)

These figures, however, are not only puzzling—their symbolism has never been satisfactorily explained—but superfluous. They clutter up the composition and make it appear "busy." Again Michelangelo included too much. There is no single point of view; pagan and Christian elements are mixed, not compounded.

Furthermore, the work, for all its superb draughtsmanship, has a touch of primitiveness about it. Michelangelo depended upon line for the definition of his forms. He had not progressed, as Leonardo da Vinci had, to represent form in values of light and shade—the chiaroscuro which was the old master's great contribution to painting. The figures of the *Doni Holy Family* appear sculptured rather than painted. They are isolated from the atmosphere, not a part of it. Hence, they seem harsh and precise, not as figures appear to the eye in life.

Because Michelangelo never forsook this linear style of painting he somewhat deserves the comment of El Greco: "Michelangelo was such a great painter, it is a pity that he never learned to paint." From the point of view of technique, Michelangelo's paintings are inferior to those of Leonardo da Vinci and to those of later but still contemporary artists, particularly Titian. Michelangelo, however, firmly maintained that he was no painter, and resented assignments to paint. He greatly respected Titian, but he stubbornly refused to learn, as Titian did, from his rival Leonardo da Vinci.

Michelangelo was superior to Leonardo, however, in that he was a fine colorist, conscious of the reflections and reverberations that color can bring to form. In the *Doni Holy Family* the color plays on the fully modeled figures as light plays on a piece of sculpture, increasing its dimensions of meaning. Hence the figures appear more sculptured in the round than painted on a flat, two-dimensional surface. To the sharp tones of St. Joseph's slate-blue and orange robes, for example, are contrasted the rose and azure of the Virgin's garments. Between the rose and the orange is the bronze hue of the Child's skin. These contrasts in luminous tone increase the sculptural sense of the work.

In spite of its faults the *Doni Holy Family* reminded everyone in Florence that Michelangelo at the outset of his career had been a painter and had by no means lost his talent in that field of art. The painting alone, not to mention the triumphant unveiling of the *David*, raised Michelangelo's reputation to such a peak that he may even have demanded of the signoria the right to fresco a wall of the council chamber of their palace. At any rate, Piero Soderini, who had taken office as gonfalonier for life on November 1, 1502, gave Michelangelo a contract for the wall in August, 1504, and assigned him a workshop in which to prepare a cartoon for the fresco.

The cartoon was a drawing on paper backed with linen, in the exact dimensions of the painting to be made from it. The cartoon would be placed in sections on the wall. Then powdered charcoal would be rubbed over its perforated outlines in order to transfer them to the surface for the guidance of the painter. For fresco painting has to be done on wet plaster, a small area at a time, and cannot be well worked over or even touched up.

The theme of the fresco for the council chamber was to be a military victory of Florence. Nearly a year earlier, in October, 1503, Leonardo da Vinci had been commissioned to decorate the opposite wall with a Florentine military victory. He had chosen the Battle of Anghiari, at which the Florentines had triumphed over the Milanese in 1440, and had begun work on it in the spring of 1504. Hence, Michelangelo could see him at work and surreptitiously borrow a few of the more experienced master's ideas. Always an experimenter, however, Leonardo

(a)

(b)

Copies by Marcantonio Raimondi (a) and Antonio Veneziano (b) of
Michelangelo's cartoon for the Battle of Cascina (Uffizi, Florence)

painted his wall of the council chamber in encaustic (wax paint), and thirty years later his battle scene had so deteriorated that it had to be scrubbed off.

Michelangelo chose for his subject a moment before the Battle of Cascina, in which Florence defeated Pisa in 1364. The day being hot, over three quarters of the Florentine soldiers had gone swimming in the Arno. Recognizing that the army of Florence might be attacked, one of its captains dashed up to the river in mock alarm, shouting, "We are lost!" Thus he rallied the swimming soldiers back to defend their camp.

It was a subtle choice, for in 1504 another war with Pisa was imminent. It also gave Michelangelo a chance to attempt a transfer of his vast knowledge of anatomy and volume from sculpture to painting, for naturally the soldiers he· depicted scrambling up the riverbank from their swim and struggling into their clothes and armor were nude males.

Michelangelo never reproduced his cartoon of the *Battle of Cascina* on the wall of the council chamber. Judging from the dimensions of Leonardo's cartoon, which must have been of approximately equal size since it was destined for a matching wall, it covered 288 square feet of paper. Hence, what we know of it is but a small section, probably the right-hand one of three panels. For, like Leonardo's, the work has vanished. Copies of both designs, however, have survived.

A copy of Michelangelo's cartoon shows a group of interlocking male nudes which recalls Michelangelo's early bas-relief, the *Battle of the Centaurs* (page 27). Later Michelangelo would say: "The more a painting resembles sculpture, the better picture it is." The *Battle of Cascina* is really a study of male anatomy in action. There is, however, considerable psychology expressed in the different ways the soldiers are responding to the alarm. Some are concerned only with themselves; others are helping their comrades; one old man is in a fury of frustration as he tries to pull his tight leather leggings over his wet limbs. Again time has been arrested for a moment, and past, present, and future have been captured.

Hundreds of artists studied Michelangelo's cartoon, for it was considered "the art school of the world." These students cut it up and disappeared with the fragments. They might have done better to study Leonardo's *Battle of Anghiari* (a copy of which by Peter Paul Rubens is in the Louvre), for that more mature work contains a symbolism that raises it artistically above Michelangelo's storytelling.

Michelangelo at least began several other works during this stay of his in Florence. Perhaps the earliest is the *Madonna and Child* now in the Church of Notre Dame, Bruges, Belgium, and hence known as the "Bruges Madonna." This small (49.21 inches high) marble is so close in spirit to the *Pietà* in St. Peter's that Michelangelo may have conceived it soon after finishing that more famous work. Its style, however, is more challenging and less tender; some of the vigor of the *David* has crept into this simple and touching statue. It may have been executed in the autumn of 1505; at any rate, it was completed by August 14, 1506, at which time it was ready to be shipped to Bruges, where it had been bought by the merchants Giovanni and Alessandro Moscheroni (or Mouscrons).

The Virgin of the Bruges Madonna sits lost in thought, as if brooding over what she has been reading in the book she holds in her right hand. The Child is tentatively stealing away from her knee. He is an infant not yet completely sure of his little legs; his right foot stretches for solid ground on which to get his balance, while he still grasps his mother's left hand to steady himself. As in the *Madonna of the Stairs,* the mother here seems remote and detached, but the lines of her arms and knees circle around the Child in a kind of protecting envelope. The group seems to express the wistfulness a mother feels when she

The *Bruges Madonna* (Notre Dame, Bruges)

sees her children leaving her to set out more and more on their own toward an uncertain future.

A marble tondo, commissioned by the Florentine merchant Taddeo Taddei, and hence known as the *Taddei Madonna*, also belongs to this period of Michelangelo's life. It is now in the Royal Academy, London. Probably it was executed at approximately the same time (1503–4) as the *Doni Holy Family*, or soon thereafter, for there is a close relationship between that painting and the small (forty-inch diameter) bas-relief. Also, the influence of Leonardo da Vinci is strong in the *Taddei Madonna*, especially in the pose of the infant Christ.

In this tondo, Michelangelo left the figures still emerging from the marble, much of which is rough-cut. Only the head of the Virgin and the figure of the Child are fully executed. This deliberate "unfinished" technique gives the work the quality of a sketch. Also, the Virgin and St. John are presented in profile. Hence, the spectator tends to become more involved in the little drama than if it were completely defined. It is a charming anecdote of childhood, for the Infant Christ is frightened by the bird that His older cousin holds out to Him, and is running to the safety of His mother's arms. Meanwhile the Virgin smiles patiently and gratefully at the well-intentioned gift from her Son's playmate.

Twenty-two-year-old Raphael Sanzio saw the tondo in Taddeo Taddei's house and made a careful drawing of it. From this, in 1505, he developed his *Madonna of the Goldfinch*, in the Uffizi Gallery, Florence. Michelangelo learned of Raphael's adaptation of his own work and forever afterward despised the younger artist as a plagiarist. Actually Raphael was honoring Michelangelo, who was only eight years older than he, but Michelangelo did not interpret Raphael's borrowing in that way. "Whatever he had of art he got from me" was Michel-

The *Taddei Madonna* (Royal Academy, London)

angelo's later judgment on his brilliant rival. Raphael's retort
was that Michelangelo was friendless for good reason—he liked
no one and no one liked him. The gregarious Raphael nicknamed Michelangelo "the hangman" to indicate how he was,
and should be, shunned. The two great contemporaries were
enemies until Raphael's untimely death at the age of thirty-
seven.

Michelangelo's annoyance at being imitated—he ordered his
father to have the Bruges Madonna locked up so that no one
could copy it—was his way of concealing his own indebtedness
to contemporary artists. His debt to Leonardo da Vinci is clear;
he also owed many ideas to Luca Signorelli. Almost the only
artists Michelangelo praised and openly admired were young
followers of his, most of whom were vastly inferior.

During his four years in Florence, Michelangelo was offered
and accepted more commissions than he could possibly execute.
Obviously he could not resist making the most of the recognition he had gained. His failure to fulfill his contracts sometimes
troubled his conscience, and he made some attempts to do the
work he had promised. If such assignments proved uninterest-
ing or demanded a backward step, however, he utterly neglected them. Time was at his back, constantly prodding him
on to accomplish what his ever-expanding vision revealed to
him.

Another reason for Michelangelo's neglect of assignments
was the effort he was putting, at this time, into the study of
poetry and of writing poetry. He may have begun versifying in
the days of his study under Ghirlandaio and Bertoldo, for from
them he would have learned the inseparable connection between art and literature. In Lorenzo de' Medici's household he
was continually exposed to poetry, both the lofty epics of
Poliziano and the more popular lyrics of Pulci and Lorenzo
himself. His sojourn with Aldovrandi in Bologna exposed him

to the poets his host patronized. Back in Florence again, Michelangelo was in a nest of poets, many of whom were writing verses about his sculptures. "There was not a literary man in Florence," Michelangelo wrote, "who was not my friend." He discovered that the creative process is the same, whether the result is a painting, a statue, or a poem. His powerful creative urge drove him to give form to ideas through words as well as through paint or marble.

Once Michelangelo had found this additional means of expressing himself on the one hand, and of enriching and freeing his spirit on the other hand, he never stopped writing poetry. Of his poems that survive, the earliest date from about 1503. At that time, Michelangelo was experimenting with metrical forms (quatrains, madrigals, sonnets) and with tones (scholarly, popular, idealistic, realistic), as well as with language itself. His thought deals with nature; the power and philosophical significance of Love; passion and guilt; the origin of beauty; the power of virtue; the relationship between good and evil.

These early poems of Michelangelo's are simple, but they are by no means commonplace, even though they follow the poetical conventions of the day. The language is vigorous, and the expression is often vividly original. Later, Michelangelo's poetry, into which he put his most intimate thoughts, feelings, and meditations, would become much more complicated. Generally Michelangelo considered his poems insignificant trifles. His contemporaries, however, regarded them as excellent works of art, and even lectured on them. As a whole, they make an intensely personal portrait of the genius.

These happy, stupendously productive years in Florence came to an abrupt end in March, 1505. On the recommendation of Giuliano da Sangallo, who was now the papal architect, Pope Julius II invited Michelangelo to work for him in Rome. It was a summons which Michelangelo could not refuse. The pope was a power, and Pope Julius II, perhaps more than any of his immediate predecessors, fully exercised the title he received at his coronation: "Ruler of the World, Father of princes and of kings, Earthly Vicar of Jesus Christ our Savior."

Leaving behind him unfulfilled contracts for statues, and an uncast *David* which he had made for a French general and which disappeared about 1650, Michelangelo set out for Rome again, possibly full of high hopes, certainly unaware that he was beginning a long period of tragic disappointment.

V: PRISONERS IN STONE

The ambassador of Venice to the papal court in Rome reported of Pope Julius II: "No one has any influence over him. He consults few or none. Anything he has been thinking of overnight has to be carried out immediately the next morning, and he insists on doing everything himself. It is impossible to describe how headstrong and violent and difficult to manage he is. Everything about him is on a magnificent scale. There is nothing in him that is small or meanly selfish. Whatever is in his mind must be carried through, even if he himself were to perish in the attempt."

Giuliano della Rovere, nephew of Pope Sixtus IV, Bishop of Ostia, Cardinal of San Pietro in Vincoli (St. Peter in Chains), Pope Julius II, had been "thinking overnight" of a tomb for himself that would serve to remind future ages of the magnificent scale of his character and his achievements. Like a pharaoh of ancient Egypt he had no intention of leaving such a monument to the discretion of his survivors, but insisted that it be carried through before he himself perished.

Julius II had already determined that the ancient basilica of St. Peter, which had been in a sad state of repair for over fifty years, should be restored. He had engaged the Florentine architect Giuliano da Sangallo to superintend the restoration. The church already housed the simple tomb of St. Peter, the first pope. Consequently, it was only fitting that it should also contain the splendid tomb of St. Peter's hierarchical descendant, Pope Julius II.

This was the commission that the sixty-two-year-old Pope Julius entrusted to the thirty-year-old Michelangelo. The sculptor from Florence responded enthusiastically to the pope's grandiose ideas, and quickly produced a design for the tomb. It was to be a freestanding monument (24 x 36 feet) rising in three tiers to a height of about 60 feet over an interior oval room that would contain the pope's sarcophagus. On the sides and cornices, and at the very top, were to be distributed fifty-three statues.

Once he had inspected this plan, Pope Julius could see that he had found a man whose sense of majestic grandeur surpassed even his own. The two men were similar in character—equally vigorous and energetic, equally impetuous, equally hot-tempered, equally driven by conceptions of splendid and magnificent achievements. They clashed only when the power of place, which was Julius', asserted itself against the power of genius, which was Michelangelo's.

In April, 1505, Michelangelo set out for Carrara to supervise the cutting of the tons of marble blocks he would need to execute his design for the tomb of Julius II. There in the mountains overlooking the sea he stayed until mid-November, dreaming again of the colossus he hoped some day to release with his chisel from the marble crags he saw imprisoning it.

During these months of relative inactivity in Carrara, Michelangelo probably completed the Bruges Madonna. Then, after a short stay in Florence, probably for the purpose of delivering the *Madonna* and of enlisting helpers for the tomb, he returned to Rome in December, 1505. By that time, some of the marble from Carrara had arrived. Eventually it was a quantity so great that, says Condivi, "when it was all spread out upon the square [before St. Peter's], it stirred amazement in the minds of most folk, but joy in the Pope's."

Michelangelo began to work on these blocks in his lodging. This probably was on the present Via de' Corridori. It is described as having been close to the covered way, built in 1410 to connect the pope's palace, the Vatican, with the Castel Sant' Angelo (Hadrian's mausoleum). The popes then used that monumental tomb as a fortress to which they could escape in times of trouble. In order to visit Michelangelo easily, the pope had a drawbridge built from his own palace to the sculptor's studio. There Julius II would inspect his sculptor's progress and discuss the work that he and his brothers were planning for Michelangelo to accomplish in the future.

The tomb was not only a stupendous challenge for the sculptor but also an opportunity for him to display his genius to subsequent ages. Had it ever been finished as it was originally planned, it would have been one of the wonders of the world, surpassing perhaps even the fabled mausoleum of Halicarnassus. The gradual diminishing of the design, the reduction in scale, the delays and disappointments that went on for forty years constituted what Condivi calls "the tragedy of the tomb" —a bitter blow to Michelangelo's aspirations and a sad example of the way in which petty affairs of the moment can defeat projects of grandeur and permanence.

Michelangelo kept the pope in good humor by outlining his glorious ideas for the tomb while both men waited for the rest of the marble to come by boat from Carrara, and for Michelangelo's assistants to come from Florence. Michelangelo had given his clothes to his father and brothers; he was happy in Rome this time, and he appears to have had no thought of returning to Florence permanently.

Rome was then a different city from the turbulent capital it was under the Borgia Pope Alexander VI, when Michelangelo had been homesick there. In the three years of Julius II's pontificate Rome had become more orderly and more cosmopolitan. At the Della Rovere pope's bidding, artists had flocked to Rome to construct and decorate the buildings with which he was adorning the city. There was intense rivalry and intrigue among these artists for getting a papal commission.

Michelangelo spent a good deal of his free time with Giuliano da Sangallo and his family. With him and the architect's young son, Francesco, Michelangelo hastened early one January morning in 1506 to the vineyard of Felis de Fredis to see the *Laocoön* group that had just been discovered there in a chamber of Nero's buried Golden House. This splendid Greek marble group, now in the Vatican Museum—Julius II bought it for his collection of antiquities—was to have considerable influence on Michelangelo.

Then trouble began. Donato Bramante, a painter and architect from Urbino, and uncle of the painter Raphael, was an intriguer. Being a skillful courtier, he gained the ear of Pope Julius II, and persuaded him that the crumbling remains of St. Peter's should be completely demolished. The pope should then commission him to build an entirely new church, one that would have no equal for splendor in the entire world. The idea appealed strongly to the grandeur-loving Julius.

Michelangelo, who was too brusque to be a courtier and who had no liking for the maneuvering that went on in courts, protested. He had already determined that the tomb of Julius II should be located in the recently rebuilt choir of St. Peter's, and he could see that Bramante's proposal would mean a delay of many years before the tomb could be erected anywhere within the church. Michelangelo's objections irritated Bramante, who wanted to get rid of all adherents of his predecessor, Giuliano da Sangallo. Sangallo had retired as architect of the basilica after the pope had preferred Bramante's plans for the church to his. Consequently Bramante began to discredit Michelangelo to the pope.

Julius II, completely wrapped up in this new project for St. Peter's and in his plans for subduing Bologna and adding it to the papal states which he was busily consolidating, began to lose interest in the tomb. To the pragmatic pope, first things came first. He was not dead yet, and he was impressed with Bramante's insidious argument that building a tomb within his lifetime was sure to bring bad luck. Julius II decided to spend not a penny more on marble for Michelangelo.

Michelangelo heard the pope voice this decision to Johannes Burchard, his master of ceremonies, on April 11, the day before Easter, 1506. Since Michelangelo had borrowed money from Jacopo Gallo's bank to pay for the marbles that had arrived from Carrara, had imported stonemasons from Florence, and had furnished his house to accommodate them in Rome, he was, as he himself said, "much embarrassed without money."

On that Holy Saturday, Michelangelo asked the pope for part of the money he needed to continue his work on the tomb. The pope told him to come back on Monday.

"I returned on Monday," Michelangelo wrote to Sangallo, "and on Tuesday and on Wednesday and on Thursday, as he [Pope Julius II] was aware. Finally on Friday morning I was turned out; in other words, I was sent packing."

On that Friday morning, the palace servant, who was so rudely preventing Michelangelo from seeing the pope, was interrupted by Julius' nephew, Cardinal Galleoto Franciotti, Bishop of Lucca.

"Don't you know who this man is?" asked the astonished cardinal.

"Pardon me, sir," replied the groom, "these are my orders." And he shoved Michelangelo out of the Vatican.

Michelangelo went back to his house "behind Santa Caterina" in a fury. There he wrote to the pope: "Most Blessed Father, I was turned out of the palace this morning by order of Your Holiness. I must therefore inform you that from now on, if You want me, You must seek me elsewhere than in Rome."

Michelangelo sent the letter off on April 17. Then he instructed his assistants to sell the contents of his house to a secondhand furniture dealer, and jumped into the mail coach for Florence.

He had got as far as Poggibonsi, twenty-six miles south of Florence, when five horsemen whom the pope had sent after him caught up with him about ten o'clock at night. They gave him a letter from Julius II: "Immediately on receipt of this, return to Rome, upon pain of Our displeasure."

The horsemen requested a reply from Michelangelo by way of a receipt for the pope's letter.

"Tell him," Michelangelo said, "that whenever he discharges his obligations to me, I will return. Otherwise he can never hope to get me back."

On the following morning Michelangelo finished his journey to Florence. There he nursed his rage over the insult he had received and over being swindled out of a sizable sum of money. At least he had done what few men dared to do—defy the supreme pontiff of Christendom. And he was safe from assassination in Florence; fear that Bramante would use hired daggers to rid himself of his rival had been one of the motives for Michelangelo's flight from Rome. "I had cause to think," he wrote to Sangallo on May 2, 1506, "that if I remained in Rome, my own tomb would be made sooner than the Pope's."

By the date of that letter Michelangelo had calmed down enough to instruct Sangallo to tell the pope that he would willingly continue the work on the tomb and finish it within the five years stipulated in the contract. "I have promised," Michelangelo added, "that . . . there will be nothing to equal it the world over." He made the condition, however, that the pope would have to let him work on it in Florence and also pay him what was due him then and on completion of the work. Living was less expensive in Florence, and the working conditions better there than in Rome.

Pope Julius, however, would accept no compromises. He kept sending orders to the signoria of Florence to have them return Michelangelo to him. Probably delighted at the defiance of their fellow citizen, the legislators of Florence ignored these demands. And the pope ignored Michelangelo's conditions.

Michelangelo passed the summer of 1506 in work on two commissions he had accepted during his previous stay in Florence. One of these was a tondo for the rich Florentine merchant Bartolommeo Pitti. This small (thirty-two inches in diameter) marble, known as the *Pitti Madonna*, is now in the Bargello in Florence.

Here a monumental Virgin sits gazing at the spectator with a look of prophecy. Her left arm embraces a relaxed and dreamy Child, who leans His right elbow on the book His mother has been showing Him and seems to be looking at the pictures in it. A young St. John, dimly sketched in the marble, looks over the Virgin's left shoulder. The Virgin's eyes seem to glimpse him. Michelangelo thus indicates the relationship between the herald of salvation (St. John the Baptist) and the Savior Himself.

Both the solid cube on which the Virgin sits, and her heroic-size head, break into the frame around the edge of the roundel, stabilizing the dynamic whirl of the circular composition. The rough, "unfinished" background and the incompletely carved parts of the figures give the work an atmosphere of its own, out of which dramatically emerge the strong, high modeling of the Virgin's head, her left knee, and the head and torso of the Child. This emergence of the forms suggests a struggle on the part of

The *Pitti Madonna* (Bargello, Florence)

the creator to give birth to his conception. The *Pitti Madonna* exhibits the terrible tensions of the sculptor as he labored to free his figures from the rock and liberate his visions into meaningful form.

The same strength and the same tensions appear in the *St. Matthew,* which Michelangelo also worked on in Florence during the summer and fall of 1506. This is the only one of the statues of the twelve apostles that he even began in fulfillment of a contract he had signed with the operai of the Cathedral of Florence on August 24, 1503. He was to have furnished one statue a year; meanwhile he was to be paid, in addition to his fee, for costs of living and for assistants. The operai also built him a house in the Borgo Pinti, which he occupied free of charge, whenever he was in Florence, until 1508.

The *St. Matthew,* now in the Academy of Fine Arts, Florence, is a mighty figure surging out of stone. The form itself is little more than a shadow, but it throbs with life as if it were taking part in its own liberation from the marble. The gnarled face of the saint, sketchy as it is, has the awesome look of a soul in agony. The whole writhing figure suggests the battle between spirit and matter. The huge size of the block—eight and a half feet high—lends a cosmic dimension to St. Matthew's torment; he is the eternal individual fighting like a champion the forces that would destroy his individuality. The work is a superb expression of man's spirit.

The *St. Matthew* is also a revelation of Michelangelo's personality at the time—a profound psychological portrait of the artist. It is a fine example of Michelangelo's artistic creed as he stated it in one of his sonnets:

> The best of artists has no concept
> Not already held within the shell

St. Matthew (Academy of Fine Arts, Florence)

> Of a stone block. He reaches it
> Only when his hand follows the guidance
> of his mind and soul.

Michelangelo frequently used the word *intelletto*, translated above as "mind and soul" rather than, literally, as "intellect." By this word he seems to mean, on the one hand, perception through the five senses. On the other hand, he means an interior perception of a higher degree—the recognition of the divine essence of life in all living things. Stone, to Michelangelo, was definitely "living." It appeared to him as the body of so-called inanimate nature enclosing a soul, an idea, that the sculptor's chisel reveals and interprets.

This sonnet was the subject of Benedetto Varchi's lecture to the Florentine Academy one Lenten Sunday in 1546. Varchi commented that artistic creation is the translation of the potential to the actual. He meant—and so did Michelangelo—that form is predetermined. It exists in the mind of God which man shares insofar as he strives toward perfection.

By "artists" Michelangelo means creators. In the sonnet he is clearly thinking of a sculptor, but he applied the same theory to a painter. "Fine painting," he said, "is nothing more than a copy of the perfections of God and a remembrance of His painting, and lastly a music and a melody that only the intellect can hear—with great difficulty."

The violent striving of *St. Matthew*, therefore, seems to express the "great difficulty" with which the artist struggles against the limitations of human imperfection and discord to remember the perfection and to hear the music and the melody.

The *St. Matthew* also shows Michelangelo's methods of work. In the beginning was his highly individualistic conception of the work—what he called "the image of the heart." Nothing is known factually of this apostle except that he was a rich tax-collector who "made a great feast" in his own house in honor of Jesus. The legends of St. Matthew's missions after the Ascension indicate that he was a man of action, a resolute debater, and fearless even when about to be eaten by canni-bals—as he seems eventually to have been. By representing Matthew as a rugged old man in a contorted posture, Michel-angelo, working from the "facts," expresses his own vision of the saint as a man struggling for his very life to turn the savage, hostile heathen into the way of eternal life that Christ died to give to them. The only conventional attribute of Michelan-gelo's *St. Matthew* is the book the figure holds, signifying his authorship of the gospel known by his name.

The next step in Michelangelo's creative process was to make "notes" of his concept. These were usually sketches set down in a kind of artistic shorthand. They seem done in a frenzy of excitement as the artist strove to translate his inner perception into outer form. Vasari called the tension that produced them "the fury of art."

Sometimes a wax model took the place of the rapid sketches; sometimes both show the externalization of Michelangelo's thoughts. Often both sketches and models developed into larger, grander proportions and freer form. Finally they became detailed studies.

The detailed studies came into contact with the material itself. First Michelangelo hewed his block of stone into general-ized organic shape. This procedure changed the rigid geometry of the original block into a form that had, as it were, a flexibility and organic life of its own.

On this "animated" block Michelangelo drew the outline of his figure on the front, and if it was to be a figure in the round, on the sides and back as well. Using a punch, he picked out the drawn outline. Then with a gradin he went down to the deeper levels. The gradin left a diagonal hatching on the marble which

emphasized by contrast the plastic modeling of the upper sur-
faces.

Michelangelo worked on the entire figure at once, using both
of his hands with equal facility. In order to see all parts of the
figure in relation to one another, he would place the wax model
in a tub of water. As he raised it gradually above the surface, he
could see what parts emerged first. From those he worked to the
lower ones, which, though submerged, he could see through the
transparent water. Hence, he could imagine them "submerged"
in the marble.

At each stage of his carving, therefore, Michelangelo produced a true work of art. He could stop at any one of these
stages. Therefore, many of his works are intentionally "unfinished," yet complete.

The St. Matthew, however, was probably set aside owing to
complications in Michelangelo's life. Once he had sketched its
form and liberated it from the stone, he never came back to it.
Other works he did return to from time to time, working on one
layer or another until he had brought the whole close to perfection.

Pope Julius II had not given up trying to get Michelangelo
back into his service. Early in May, 1506, he instructed Sangallo, who was going from Rome to Florence, to bring Michelangelo back to Rome with him. The pope had decided that
Michelangelo should paint the ceiling of the Sistine Chapel in
the Vatican, a plan that Bramante vigorously opposed. Bramante not only wanted Michelangelo out of the way, but also
wanted his nephew Raphael to get the job of decorating the
vault of the Sistine Chapel.

Knowing that the pope heartily wished Michelangelo to
return, Michelangelo's friends urged him to do so for the sake
of his prestige and his personal honor. Michelangelo, however,
was still in terror of what might happen to him in Rome

through vindictiveness on the part of Bramante or some other foe. When, on July 8, 1506, Julius II issued to the Florentine signoria a second demand to send Michelangelo to him, Piero Soderini replied that the sculptor would not budge without a signed letter guaranteeing his safety and immunity. Otherwise, Michelangelo seemed willing enough to go, for the pope had promised to restore him to full "apostolic favor."

Then on August 27, 1506, Julius II launched a military campaign to "free" Perugia and Bologna from their despotic rulers and add these rich cities to the papal states for their own benefit and protection. He himself led his army of twenty-four cardinals and five hundred soldiers, who were later reinforced by French troops. Perugia surrendered, and on November 10, Pope Julius made a triumphal entry into Bologna. The bold, swift campaign struck terror into the governments of other cities of the peninsula.

Consequently, when, on November 21, Pope Julius made a third demand on the signoria to extradite Michelangelo, Piero Soderini put personal pressure on his sculptor friend to go to the pope at Bologna.

"You have tried a bout with the pope," Soderini told Michelangelo, "on which the king of France would not have ventured. Therefore, you must not go on letting yourself be requested. We do not wish to go to war with him on your account, and put our state in peril. Make up your mind to return."

Michelangelo still feared for his personal safety. The requested letter of safe-conduct had not arrived. He replied to Soderini that if Florence would no longer shelter him, then he would accept an invitation from the sultan of Turkey to build a bridge over the Hellespont.

Soderini counseled him that death at the hands of the pope would be better than life with the heathen Turks, and agreed to send him to Bologna as an ambassador of Florence, hence immune to violence or punishment.

Armed with this diplomatic passport, Michelangelo set out for Bologna on November 28, 1506. Hence, the *St. Matthew* was not finished, nor was the cartoon of the *Battle of Cascina* on which Michelangelo had resumed work. Soderini's letters of safe-conduct indicate the great sacrifice Florence was making by granting the pope's wish to regain Michelangelo's services.

Scared to death when he arrived in Bologna the next day, Michelangelo took the precaution of going to early mass at the Church of San Petronio before facing Pope Julius II, into whose presence he was brought while the pontiff was still at breakfast.

Michelangelo had put a halter around his neck as a symbol of humility. He fell on his knees before the pope and loudly besought pardon. He protested that his hasty departure from Rome seven months before had been caused by his distress at having been put out of the Vatican. He had not, he insisted, acted out of insolence or pride.

A bishop interceded for the groveling sculptor. "Your Holiness," said the prelate, "he did wrong through ignorance. These painters, outside their art, are all like this."

Pope Julius turned his fury on this interfering churchman. "It's you who are ignorant," he shouted, striking at the bishop with his mace. "You have insulted him in a way We would not dream of. Get out of my sight, and bad luck to you!"

A servant drove the bishop out of the palace with blows and kicks.

Once his flurry of temper was over Pope Julius pardoned Michelangelo and gave him his blessing. This was all Michelangelo needed—encouragement and affection. In Piero Soderini's letter of introduction to his brother Francesco, Cardinal of

Volterra, which Michelangelo had taken with him to Bologna, he had written: "His nature is such that with encouragement and kindness he will do anything. Show him courtesy and affection, and he will accomplish things that will astonish the beholder."

Pope Julius had learned his lesson. From then on, he was careful not to go too far with Michelangelo. Actually, the pope loved him more than anyone else in the papal entourage.

To commemorate his victory in the campaign that everyone had thought would prove a disaster, Julius II ordered Michelangelo to make a gigantic statue of him that he would leave in subjugated Bologna. For fifteen months Michelangelo remained in that city working on it.

Bologna was jammed with the pope's retinue, members of the new papal government, and the soldiers of the papal army of occupation. Julius II did not return to Rome until February 22, 1507. Michelangelo could get only one room to house himself and the two craftsmen he had imported from Florence to help him work on the pope's statue. His faithful *garzone,* Piero d'Argenta, was also part of the team. The four had to sleep in one bed. This was not an uncommon practice, especially in inns, for sixteenth-century beds were built for many occupants, but it must have been distinctly uncomfortable, especially in the unusually hot summer of 1507. Michelangelo, however, had a workshop in the Stanza del Pavaglione, behind the cathedral.

One of the Florentine assistants had to be dismissed for dishonesty and insubordination, and he persuaded the other to leave. Plague broke out in crowded Bologna. The cost of living was very high, as it was wherever the pope was. The Bolognese nobles were fomenting a rebellion against the papal government. Michelangelo worked on the statue of the pope only to get back into Julius' favor; otherwise he was displeased with everything about the project.

The first casting of the statue into bronze turned out badly. Michelangelo wrote home of his extreme fatigue. By January, 1508, he wrote that he felt he had been in Bologna a thousand years.

The whole exasperating experience heated Michelangelo's temper and honed his razorlike tongue. When the Bolognese painter and bronze worker Francia visited the sculptor to inspect the statue, he naturally admired the beauty of the casting and of the bronze that Michelangelo was then polishing.

"I owe as much to Pope Julius, who gave me the bronze," Michelangelo snapped at the much older man, "as you owe to the chemists who gave you your colors for painting."

Then he called Francia a fool.

Later, when Francia's handsome son was introduced to him, Michelangelo said: "Your father makes better living figures than painted ones."

On the afternoon of February 21, 1508, with great ceremony and acclaim, the bronze statue of Pope Julius II was set up over the central door in the facade of the Church of San Petronio. Michelangelo's net profit for the entire tremendous undertaking was only four and a half ducats. The pope, however, was very pleased with the result.

The statue remained in place only until December 30, 1511. On that day the party of the Bentivogli, the former rulers of Bologna, actively rebelled against the pope. They threw down Michelangelo's ten-foot-high statue of Julius II, and shipped it off to Ferrara to be melted down for a cannon. All that is known of the statue is that the pope was represented seated, in full pontifical regalia, holding the keys of St. Peter in his left hand, and raising his right hand in benediction.

The keys were apparently a compromise. The pope had seen the clay model of the statue and enthusiastically approved it except for the posture of the figure's hands.

"Is the right hand supposed to be delivering a blessing or a curse?" asked the pope.

"Your Holiness," replied Michelangelo, "is admonishing the people of Bologna to behave sensibly."

The pope then asked what was to go in his left hand.

"A book," Michelangelo told him.

"Put a sword there," ordered the pope, who was much pleased over his unexpected military triumph. "I know nothing about reading."

His ordeal in Bologna over, Michelangelo returned to Florence in late February, 1508. Piero Soderini immediately approached him to do a statue of Hercules, equal in size to his *David*, for the side of the palace of the signoria opposite that colossus. But before Michelangelo could even get the marble for it, Pope Julius II had sent for him to come to Rome. He must have left Florence shortly after March 13, for on that day he became legally free from his father's control over his person and his property. He was then one week past the age of thirty-three.

VI: THE POPE AND
THE PAINTER

The papal brief summoning Michelangelo to Rome doubtless meant to the artist that Julius II intended to have him continue his work on the pontiff's tomb. For at least two years, however, Julius had been planning to assign to Michelangelo the decoration of the vault of the Sistine Chapel in the Vatican.

This chapel, dedicated to the Mother of God, had been built between 1471 and 1483 at the command of Julius' uncle, Pope Sixtus IV—hence the name "Sistine." It is a single, solemn, grandiose hall, 133 feet long and 43 feet wide. The top of the barrel-vaulted ceiling is 68 feet above the floor of marble mosaic. A beautiful screen by Mino da Fiesole and others divides the chapel into a larger choir and a smaller nave. Twelve narrow, arched windows under the vault and high above the floor light the Sistine Chapel.

In Pope Sixtus IV's time the long walls of the chapel had been painted with frescoes depicting scenes in the life of Moses and of Christ by the most famous artists of that day. The niches between the windows contained fresco portraits of twenty-eight early popes. The ceiling vault itself, however, was merely tinted a light blue and sprinkled with yellow stars. This sparse element of decoration Pope Julius II considered inadequate.

Michelangelo's two years' absence from the Vatican had

given Bramante, a competent fresco painter himself, and his clique plenty of opportunity to discredit him as a painter. Bramante had even told the pope that Michelangelo had stated that he did not know enough about painting to take on the assignment of the Sistine Chapel. When Pope Julius returned to Rome from Bologna, delighted with having arranged Michelangelo's return to his service, the courtiers changed the pattern of their intrigue. Now they praised Michelangelo to the skies and practically insisted that he be given the ceiling. Their strategy was that due to lack of experience he would certainly fail and then would be permanently out of favor with the most powerful patron of them all. They also persuaded the pontiff that completing the decoration of the Sistine Chapel would be a more fitting memorial to the whole Della Rovere family than a tomb for Julius himself, which, they kept insisting, was a bad-luck project anyway.

Pope Julius made up his mind. None of Michelangelo's protests that he was a sculptor, not a painter, had any effect upon him. Shaping marble was like slicing butter compared to altering a decision of Pope Julius II's. Michelangelo nicknamed him Medusa, meaning that the pope had turned him into stone and implying that Julius' will was releasing form from him as he himself once freed it from living marble.

Michelangelo had seen Pope Julius' rage. He recognized that if he protested any longer, the pope would turn that fury upon him. He consented.

From a letter that Michelangelo wrote fifteen years later it appears that his first design for the ceiling was "for twelve Apostles in the lunettes [the crescent-shaped spaces above the windows] and the usual ornamentations [squares and medallions] to fill the remaining area." The idea for that design must have originated with the pope. It would seem, however, that once Michelangelo had truly studied the entire space, he concluded that such meager decoration would be, as he said, "a poor affair."

Michelangelo reported this opinion to the pope, who asked him to explain it.

"Because the Apostles themselves were poor," was Michelangelo's only comment.

Michelangelo must then have described his own concept of what he thought the decoration of the vault should be. As he listened to the eloquent artist giving voice to his soaring imagination, the pope, by no means unimaginative himself, may have felt that before him stood no short, stocky, ugly man, but rather a messenger from another world revealing a vision of the creation of the universe as if the speaker had himself been present at the first moment of recorded time when the "Spirit of God moved upon the face of the waters." For what Michelangelo proposed was no less than giving form to the mind of God. The pope, although no reader, was certainly familiar with the first chapters of the Book of Genesis, and, although no philosopher, he could dissolve into an ecstasy of contemplation when confronted with that supreme record of the act of creation.

Then, as Michelangelo wrote, "the Pope . . . gave me a new commission to do what I liked, and said he would content me and that I should paint down to the Histories [the scenes of the life of Moses and of Christ] below."

It was not customary at that time for an artist to choose his own subject matter. A great step thus was taken in the liberation of the artist from the demands of his patron. The freedom an artist knows today began with the meeting of two mighty minds, Michelangelo's and Pope Julius II's.

Pope Julius entrusted to Bramante the scaffolding necessary for the frescoing, probably after Bramante's insistence that such construction was his province as an architect. Bramante designed a platform to be suspended on ropes from holes in the roof.

When Michelangelo saw this contraption, he immediately recognized that it would sway badly and that if the ropes gave way, he would suffer a fatal fall—and that his enemy had doubtless designed the rig with these hazards well in mind.

"How are you going to plug up those holes when the painting is finished?" Michelangelo inquired.

"We'll find a way," answered the architect, "when the time comes."

Michelangelo probably sensed a sinister tone in Bramante's reply. He went to the pope and demanded permission to reconstruct the scaffolding. Bramante appeared at the conference to justify his work, which Michelangelo told him to his face was unsatisfactory. Pope Julius probably saw Bramante's intentions as clearly as Michelangelo. At any rate, Julius decided the matter in Michelangelo's favor, a verdict that hardly improved the relationship between the conniving architect and the forthright painter-sculptor.

Michelangelo hired an impoverished carpenter to erect a scaffolding on uprights clear of the walls—the design still in use today for such work, and Michelangelo's first known architectural creation. The leftover cables he gave to the carpenter, who sold them for enough money to provide his daughter with a dowry.

While this scaffolding was being built, and the ceiling replastered, Michelangelo prepared the cartoons for the mammoth project he had undertaken—ten thousand square feet of frescoing. His method was first to sketch the composition in a small scale. Next he studied portions of it from life, using his apprentices or professional male models for both male and female figures. These studies were beautifully executed in black or red chalk (crayon), or charcoal, or in pen and ink, or in wash.

At least twelve authentic examples of these detailed studies still exist; two are in the Metropolitan Museum in New York City; another, in the Institute of Arts in Detroit.

Lastly Michelangelo returned to his original composition and enlarged it into a cartoon to guide his painting.

Giuliano da Sangallo had negotiated with the pope for a price of fifteen thousand ducats for Michelangelo's work. On May 10, 1508, Michelangelo got an advance payment, which he receipted: "I, Michelangelo Buonarroti, *sculptor*, have received 500 ducats on account . . . for the *painting* on the vault of the Sistine Chapel." He was still rigidly insisting on his true calling as he saw it.

On the following day, May 11, the scaffolding began to rise in the Sistine Chapel, and the first rough coat of plaster to be applied to the ceiling.

The summer of 1508 was taken up with Michelangelo's work on the cartoons, at least one trip to Florence for the purpose of engaging assistants, with getting painting materials, and with the rebuilding of the corners of the chapel to make the concave spandrels (triangular areas) which were part of Michelangelo's design. It was certainly not before August that he began the actual painting. By January of 1509 he was deeply involved in the project, and already discouraged. On the twenty-seventh of that month he wrote to his father: "My work does not seem to me to go ahead in a way to merit [asking the pope for more money]. This is due to the difficulty of the work and also because it is not my profession. In consequence, I lose my time fruitlessly. May God help me!"

Michelangelo was probably referring to the mold that quickly formed on the panel depicting the Deluge, the first to be executed of the nine central paintings. This accident seemed enough excuse for him to give up the entire project.

"I told Your Holiness," Michelangelo complained to the

pope, "that painting is not my trade. What I have done is spoiled. If you do not believe me, send someone to inspect it."

If a painting could be so quickly obliterated by natural causes, then, Michelangelo reasoned, he was indeed losing his time fruitlessly. Here was no answer to his dream of leaving a permanent memorial to his genius, such as sculpture in stone would be.

The pope sent Giuliano da Sangallo to inspect the damage. Sangallo, being an architect and therefore familiar with construction materials, quickly diagnosed the trouble and how it could be corrected and avoided in the future. Michelangelo was doomed to continue.

Still he was miserable, probably because of diffidence over working in an alien field. "I cannot supply my own necessities," he wrote his brother Buonarroto in October, 1509. "I am living here in a state of great anxiety and of the greatest physical fatigue. I have no friends of any sort and want none."

Enthusiasm over the tremendous feat of intellectual and physical energy that produced the ceiling of the Sistine Chapel has led to many legends about the way it was achieved. One is that Michelangelo worked entirely alone on it, and in total solitude. True, the artists he imported to help him proved unworthy of the task, and he sent them back to Florence. Despite their skill in fresco painting, either they could not grasp Michelangelo's gigantic intentions or their style was not broad and free enough to execute them. Michelangelo did, however, keep several assistants, probably less individualized in their work than those he had originally engaged. The work of these lesser painters appears in several places on the ceiling. Also, Michelangelo would have needed apprentices to grind colors and prepare plaster. Not even the superhuman Michelangelo could have done everything himself and still finished the undertaking in four years.

Privacy, however, Michelangelo did insist upon. The only person he permitted to see what he was painting was Pope Julius. The pontiff could not stay away from the man he acknowledged was his counterpart in the world of art. Nor could he endure not seeing Michelangelo's progress on the scheme that had been described by the artist to him alone. Michelangelo would stop his painting long enough to help the old man up the ladders of the scaffolding. The more the pope saw of the wondrous work, the more he urged Michelangelo to hurry and complete it. Julius could not bear the thought that he might die before he had beheld the glorious monument he had commissioned.

By early August, 1510, Michelangelo had finished five of the nine panels—the eastern half—on the central vault of the Sistine Chapel ceiling. The scaffolding then had to be dismantled and reerected under the western half. The pope insisted that the public be allowed to see the finished portion. "As soon as it was thrown open," says Vasari, "the whole of Rome flocked to see it; and the Pope was the first, not having the patience to wait till the dust had settled after the dismantling of the scaffolds."

But the wonder it aroused and the awe it inspired in the spectators served to cause Bramante to renew his intrigues to get rid of Michelangelo. Bramante now proposed that his nephew Raphael, who was repainting the pope's apartments in the Vatican, now known as the "Raphael rooms," should be allowed to continue the work in the Sistine Chapel so that the chapel might be a museum of work by all the great Italian painters of the time.

Michelangelo by then had no intention of abandoning the work he had so unwillingly begun. Leading from the strength of his triumph over fresco painting thus far, he went to the pope and denounced Bramante. Michelangelo was incensed not only by his rival's persecution of him, but also by Bramante's vandalism in destroying precious elements of the old St. Peter's in order completely to reconstruct that church according to his own plans. Again Pope Julius decided for Michelangelo.

Then Pope Julius left Rome on another of his military campaigns, which kept him out of the city from August 17, 1510, to June 27, 1511. This expedition made the papal treasury too short of funds for Michelangelo to be paid for his work and reimbursed for his outlays on materials. Meanwhile, his family were, as usual, short of money. Michelangelo had to go twice to Bologna, where the pope was, in order to collect what was due him. He did not resume work on the western half of the ceiling until January, 1511.

While the scaffolding was down, Michelangelo was able at last to see from the floor the effect of the work he had done on the eastern end of the vault. He recognized that it did not adequately express his grand conception. The figures were too small, and there were, as usual, too many of them. The compositions were too busy to be easily grasped by a spectator sixty-eight feet below them.

These moments of reflection changed Michelangelo from a traditional painter with an imagination too great for his technique into a painter fully capable of executing what his mind commanded. The panel of *The Drunkenness of Noah,* for example, appeared to him—as indeed it is—actually medieval in composition; Noah is seen not only as insensible, but also as a plowman—a reminiscence of the comic-strip kind of storytelling favored by the naïve artists of the fourteenth century and earlier. The panels of the creation of the world and of man, which succeeded the earlier ones, however, are as magnificently executed as they are magnificently conceived. Nothing like them had existed before; nothing since has equaled or surpassed them.

The panels of the western section Michelangelo made more

abstract and less literal. Here is the loftiest kind of imaginative perception, and a dynamic power that seems more divine than human. For here are Michelangelo's images of the living God in the act of imperious creation—a completely human figure expressing the idea of irresistible force, mind willing matter into form.

The work went much faster now that Michelangelo felt confident of the success of his project and of the pope's trust in him. He could even laugh at his trials. In a sonnet written for a friend, Michelangelo humorously described his discomfort:

> I've got myself a goiter from this strain,
> As water gives the cats in Lombardy
> Or maybe it's in some other country;
> My belly's pushed by force beneath my chin.
>
> My beard toward Heaven, I feel the back of my brain
> Upon my neck, I grow the breast of a Harpy;
> My brush, above my face continually,
> Makes it a splendid floor by dripping down.
>
> My loins have penetrated to my paunch,
> My rump's a crupper, as a counterweight,
> And pointless the unseeing steps I go.
>
> In front of me my skin is being stretched
> While it folds up behind and forms a knot,
> And I am bending like a Syrian bow.
>
> And judgment, hence, must grow,
> Borne in the mind, peculiar and untrue;
> You cannot shoot well when the gun's askew.
>
> John, come to the rescue
> Of my dead painting now, and of my honor;
> I'm not in a good place, and I'm no painter.
>
> —tr. *Creighton Gilbert*

Michelangelo decorated the margin of this burlesque poem for Giovanni (John) da Pistoia, a comic poet himself, with a drawing of himself standing on tiptoe and reaching high above his head to paint one of the figures of the vault. This sketch should dispose of the legend that Michelangelo painted the ceiling while lying on his back.

When the pope returned from his expedition, he began pestering Michelangelo again to hurry with his work. In the early summer of 1512, Michelangelo applied to him for more money and for leave of absence to visit Florence, where he was negotiating the purchase of two farms for his ne'er-do-well brothers. The pope, who by that time knew that his days were numbered, asked him when he would finish the painting of the chapel.

"When I can," Michelangelo said, as he had often replied before.

"When I can!" roared the pope. "When I can, indeed! What do you mean? I shall make you finish it!"

Then he struck Michelangelo with his staff.

Michelangelo went directly to his house and was preparing to quit Rome for good and all again, when a messenger arrived with the pope's apologies and the money Michelangelo had requested.

Michelangelo went to Florence in June, 1512, but he was back in Rome and at work again in July. On July 24 he wrote to Buonarroto, who was impatient about getting some money from him: "I'm not well and am worn out with this stupendous labor, and yet I'm patient in order to achieve the desired end."

The desired end came on November 1, 1512. Michelangelo, having taken down all the scaffolding, opened the Sistine Chapel on that morning, and the pope sang mass beneath the glorious monument to his family that he had commissioned Michelangelo to execute.

"When the work was thrown open," says Vasari, "the whole world came running to see what Michelangelo had done; and certainly it was such as to make everyone speechless with astonishment."

The "whole world" enters the Sistine Chapel through a door at the east end, which faces the altar. Directly above them is the last panel of the narrative that begins at the western end. Proceeding, as the visitor must, these panels illustrate:

1. The Drunkenness of Noah (Genesis 9:20–23)
2. The Deluge (Genesis 7:10–24)
3. The Sacrifice of Noah (Genesis 8:20)
4. The Temptation of Eve and the Expulsion of Adam and Eve from the Garden of Eden (Genesis 3:1–24)
5. The Creation of Eve (Genesis 2:21–22)
6. The Creation of Adam (Genesis 2:7)
7. God Separates the Earth from the Waters (Genesis 1:6–10)
8. God Creates the Sun and the Moon (Genesis 1:14–16)
9. God Separates Light from Darkness (Genesis 1:3–4)

Panels 1, 3, 5, 7, and 9 are smaller than the others.

Four male nudes sit facing each other on (painted) pedestals on the north and south sides of each of the smaller panels. (One of these nudes was destroyed by fire in 1544.) They hold scarves or garlands which support bronze-colored disks. On these medallions are scenes from the Old Testament, executed as if in relief on metal.

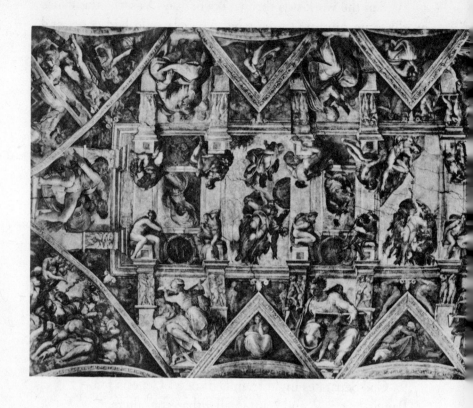

Panorama of the Sistine Chapel ceiling

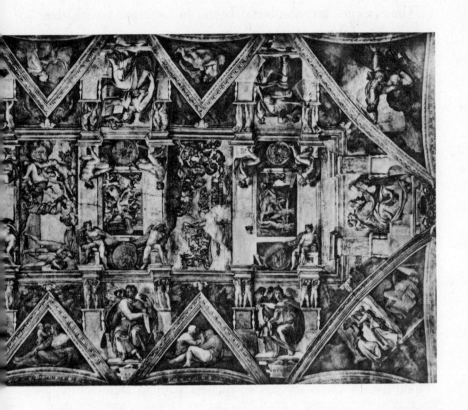

These scenes are numbered below to correspond with the numbering of the panels, as follows:

North	South
1. Joab kills Abner (II Samuel 3:27) B	Death of Joram (II Kings 9:24) A
3. Death of Uriah (II Samuel 11:9) D	Destruction of Baal's Image (II Kings 11:18) C
5. Nathan and David (II Samuel 12:1–15) F	Massacre of the Tribe of Ahab (II Chronicles 18:28–34) E
7. Death of Absalom (II Samuel 13:9) H	(Deliberately hidden in shadow of flanking figure) G
9. The Sacrifice of Isaac (Genesis 22:1–13) J	Elijah in the Chariot of Fire (II Kings 2:11) I

(Letters A through I refer to diagram on pages 120–121)

Each of the panels is flanked on the north and south sides by an Old Testament prophet or a sibyl arranged alternately. These figures sit on thrones in niches (painted architecture), and each is attended by two figures of children representing spirits or genii. Framing the thrones are pilasters (painted architecture again) on each of which are two figures of children used as telamons (columns in male human form); that is, four telamons per principal figure. Beneath the throne of each principal figure is another child, who supports the title plaque.

The Creation of Adam

The Prophet Jonah

Nude

The Brazen Serpent

Ancestors of Christ

The prophets and sibyls are, again in reference to the central panels:

North	South
1. Joel	Delphic sibyl
3. Erythraean sibyl	Isaiah
5. Ezekiel	Cumaean sibyl
7. Persian sibyl	Daniel
9. Jeremiah	Libyan sibyl

In the theology of the Renaissance, during which period the sibyls were frequently portrayed in art out of respect to classical antiquity, the sibyls are the counterparts of the prophets. The prophets link the Jewish tradition with Christianity, and the sibyls link the Greek and Roman world with Christianity. The tradition is that the sibyls, who were infinitely wise women and perhaps sorceresses to boot, foretold the coming of Christ, but there is no agreement as to what specific prophecy each one made, except that the Erythraean sibyl is generally credited with predicting the Annunciation. The sibyls were twelve in number.

At the east end, flanking the panel of *The Drunkenness of Noah*, is the prophet Zachariah; at the west end, flanking *God Separates Light from Darkness*, is the prophet Jonah.

The larger central panels are flanked by spandrels, in which are depicted, in family groups, various ancestors of Christ. All are taken from the first chapter of the Gospel according to St. Matthew. These are, in reference to the central panels:

North	South
2. Zorobabel	Josias
4. Ozias	Ezekias
6. Roboam	Asa
8. Salmon	Jesse

Below these, in the lunettes above the windows, are more ancestors of Christ, also from Matthew, as follows:

	North	*South*
East wall.	Jacob, Joseph	Eleazar, Matthan
Corner.	Achim, Eliud	Azor, Sadoc
2.	Abiud, Eliakim	Jechonias, Salathiel
4.	Joatham, Achaz	Manasses, Amon
6.	Abia	Josaphat, Joram
8.	Boaz, Obed	David, Solomon
Corner.	Aminadab	Naason

In the four corner spandrels are scenes depicting a hero or heroine of the Hebrew people delivering the children of Israel from one or another of their enemies. These are:

Southeast spandrel: Judith slaying Holofernes (Judith 12:1–15)
Southwest spandrel: The Brazen Serpent (Numbers 21:9)
Northwest spandrel: The Hanging of Haman (Esther 7:1–10)
Northeast spandrel: David Slaying Goliath (I Samuel 17:32–51)

The diagram on pages 120–121 shows the actual placement of these scenes, which contain a total of 343 figures.

The basic meaning of Michelangelo's pictorial synopsis of the world before Christ on the ceiling of the Sistine Chapel is the total involvement of God with His universe—His creation of it as an act of love; His disillusionment with man, whom He created as an extension of Himself; His redeeming love shown by the preservation of Noah and his family after the Deluge.

Michelangelo's faith in the abiding love and protection of God is what impelled him to conceive the entire work. "God did not make us to abandon us," he wrote in a letter to his father.

The cycle of the central panels leads up to the covenant God made with Noah, giving authority over the world to man, who is to be responsible to God for its government. This covenant sums up the previous two covenants God had made with man: (1) the responsibility of man to "be fruitful and multiply" and subdue the earth to human uses; (2) the hard conditions of life for man as a result of his disobedience, but with the promise of a redeemer.

The fidelity of God to that promise of redemption is illustrated in the cycle of figures and scenes that surround the central panels. The final central panel, *The Drunkenness of Noah*, leads up to that cycle. The biblical account of Noah's drunkenness ends with the prophecy that the descendants of Shem and Japheth, the sons of Noah who rebuked their brother Ham for ridiculing their father, will produce, on the one hand, divine revelation, and, on the other hand, the enlargement of man through government, science, and art. For Shem is to be the founder of the Hebrew (Semitic) people, God's chosen ones to reveal His will to the world. And Japheth is to be the founder of the people who interpret God's will in civilization.

Hence the alternation of the Hebrew prophets and the pagan sibyls along the north and south sides of the central panels. The prophets are descendants of Shem; the sibyls, of Japheth. The prophets keep man ever mindful of God's protecting and guiding love. The sibyls show man how to make God's love of practical use in man's responsibility for governing the earth. Both prophets and sibyls foretell the coming of Christ—that is, God in man—who will take away the sins of the world. Everything in the pictorial synopsis, therefore, points to that supreme

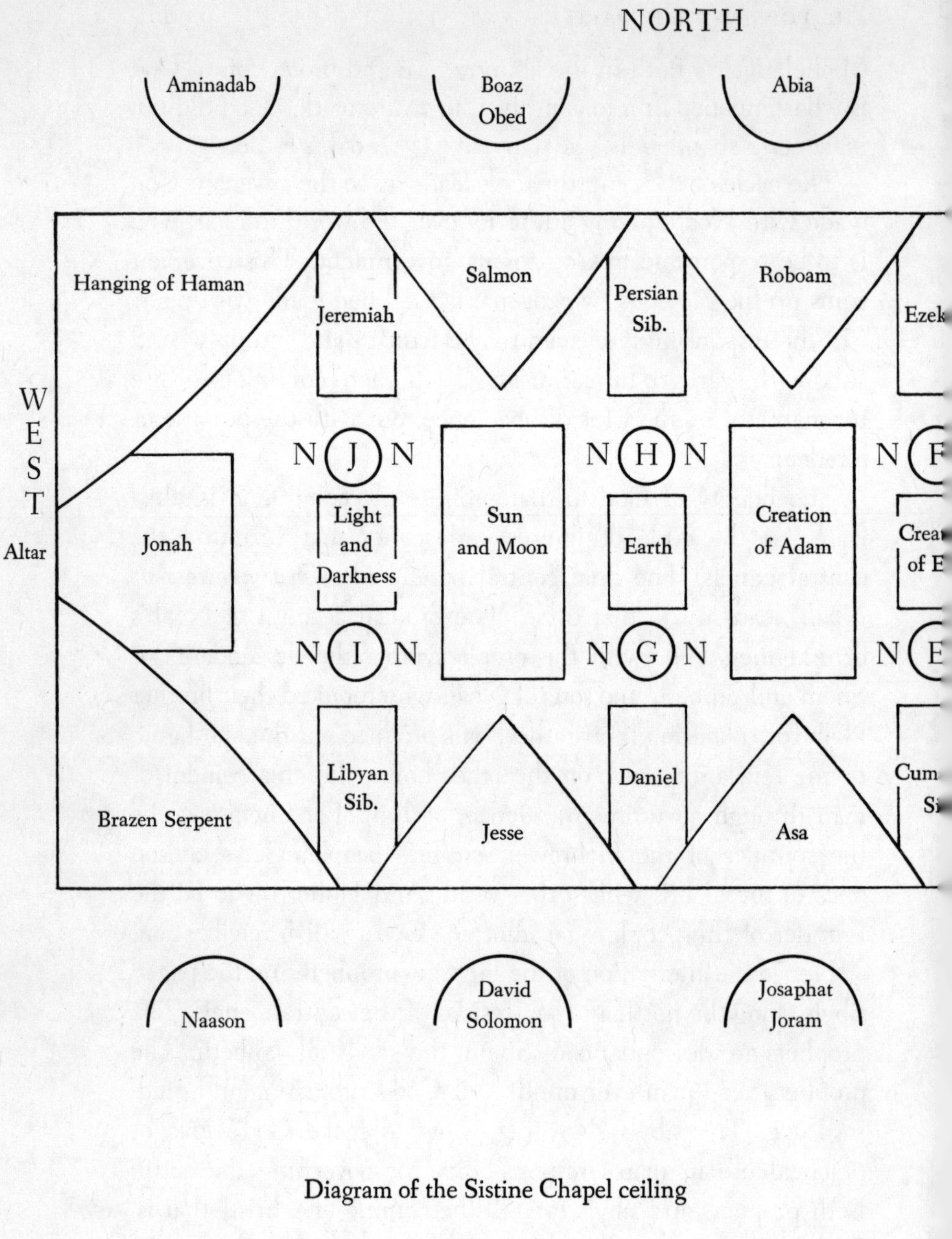

NORTH

Aminadab

Boaz
Obed

Abia

WEST

Altar

Hanging of Haman

Jeremiah

Salmon

Persian
Sib.

Roboam

Ezek

N J N

Light
and
Darkness

N H N

Sun
and Moon

Earth

Creation
of Adam

N F

Crea
of E

Jonah

N I N

N G N

N E

Libyan
Sib.

Daniel

Cum
Si

Brazen Serpent

Jesse

Asa

Naason

David
Solomon

Josaphat
Joram

Diagram of the Sistine Chapel ceiling

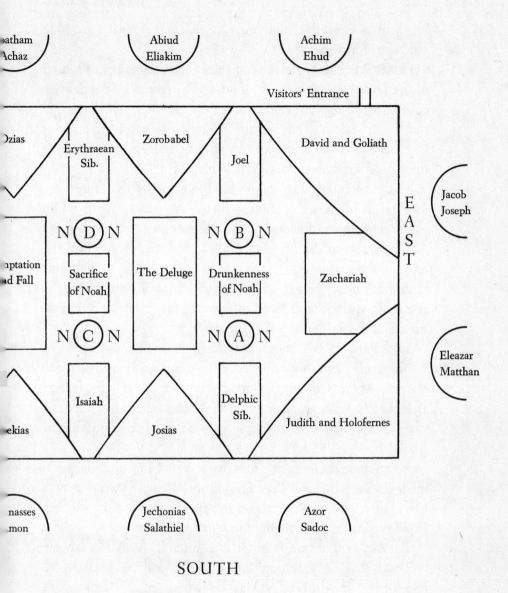

atham
Achaz

Abiud
Eliakim

Achim
Ehud

Visitors' Entrance

Ozias

Erythraean Sib.

Zorobabel

Joel

David and Goliath

E A S T

Jacob
Joseph

N D N

Sacrifice of Noah

The Deluge

N B N

Drunkenness of Noah

Zachariah

Eleazar
Matthan

nptation
d Fall

N C N

N A N

ekias

Isaiah

Josias

Delphic Sib.

Judith and Holofernes

nasses
mon

Jechonias
Salathiel

Azor
Sadoc

SOUTH

(N = Nude decorative figure, or *ignudo*)

reconciliation of God and man as the logical and inevitable outcome of history.

Hence Michelangelo's use of the human ancestors of Christ in the lateral spandrels and lunettes. The scenes of the deliverance of God's chosen people from their enemies, which occupy the corner spandrels, demonstrate God's love inspiring a savior in a time of crisis. Even woman is to be redeemed, for two of these pre-Christian saviors are Judith and Esther.

Medieval interpretation of the Bible insists that there are four levels of meaning for the incidents recorded in the Old Testament that illustrate God's relationship to his people. Those levels are the literal, the allegorical, the moral, and the mystical (or anagogical). The last two are actually dimensions or derivations of the second, the allegorical, which interprets the actual story, the literal level, in terms of mankind's redemption through the sacrifice of Jesus Christ.

Michelangelo was thoroughly familiar with these levels of meaning through his knowledge of Dante. He could recite Dante's whole *Commedia* (it was not called "Divine" until after 1555) from memory. Hence, Michelangelo intended his work on the Sistine Chapel ceiling to be interpreted on all four levels.

An attempt to clarify the first two levels of meaning has been made above. The individual himself must supply the latter two. His ability to do so depends on the effect upon him of Michelangelo's translation of thought into pictorial form.

The key to that translation is man himself, for Michelangelo believed that only through man could God be understood. Everything in the ceiling, as elsewhere in Michelangelo's works, is represented in human form. Even God the Creator is represented as a majestic old man, serene and self-contained in His realization of His own supreme power.

Man, therefore, appears on the ceiling in every imaginable attitude and every conceivable facial expression. This encyclopedia of action involves the spectator by arousing his emotions. For none of the figures is still; each is animated by a feeling of his own. This feeling, expressed in motion, calls for an emotional response from the spectator. As the spectator responds to man, so he will respond to God's intentions for man—the ultimate meaning of the work.

An invitation to the spectator to explore the moral and mystical levels of the work is the color Michelangelo used. The predominant tone is lavender, for Michelangelo disliked strong colors. "How wrong are those simpletons," he said, "who look more at a green, a red, or similar high color than at figures which show spirit and movement." At another time he said: "Poor artists cloak their poor technique with a variety of tints and colors." On the ceiling Michelangelo used no more than seven colors: white, yellow ochre, red, siena red, earth green, ultramarine blue, vine black. None of these is pure. Instead there are oranges, russet browns, cold greens, dull blues. These muted harmonies suggest the veil that hangs between things perceived only by the senses and those things as they truly exist—ideas.

The calm, forceful "architecture" of Michelangelo's ceiling also emphasizes the same sublimity. For Michelangelo enlarged the scope of the plain barrel-vault of the ceiling by adding dimensions of perspective. Hence the ceiling appears to be a kind of classical marble temple built in three levels or zones. Each of these contains one theme of the work. The "sculptured" telamons of this architecture, the cornices, the pillars, the thrones, the niches—all give an illusion of three-dimensional space. The nudes who hold the medallions, and the prophets and sibyls, therefore, seem detached from the solid wall. They sit on their blocks and their thrones in space as living persons would. The central panels are seen, as it were, through openings in the roof of the temple.

The vault therefore becomes a structure by and of itself. Each division of the "temple" has its own perspective. The whole work exists in a sphere of its own, halfway between reality and imitation. Thus it has a mystical quality in addition to a historical one.

The only fault in the work is that some of the figures and some of the details are too small to be clearly seen from the floor of the chapel.

To describe the ceiling in detail or to attempt an explanation in order to help someone to "see" it is as futile as trying to make the grandeur of the Grand Canyon or Niagara Falls felt through words alone. The mighty spirit of the work is contained in the work itself. It is an expression of intellectual energy as powerful as the divine energy depicted in it. What Michelangelo achieved—probably the greatest single achievement of any human being—is a new myth of the Creation, one that is more intelligible to modern man with his scientific approach to the formation of the universe and man himself than the fables of Genesis.

We do not see the current of life passing between the outstretched finger of God and the listlessly upraised finger of Adam in the great panel of *The Creation of Adam*. We only sense that it is there. In the same way, we sense the current of creative power passing spontaneously from the unknown, and perhaps unknowable, source of life to the hand of Michelangelo.

VII: THE TORMENTS OF TIME

After the crowds which came to view Michelangelo's masterpiece on the ceiling of the Sistine Chapel had dwindled, Michelangelo again looked critically at his great panorama of Creation. It occurred to him that the frescoes so high above the floor might be improved by some flashy touches of gold and bright blue, such as other fresco artists used at that time. The pope agreed, and urged him to add this tinsel to make the vault look richer.

Michelangelo, however, reconsidered his idea—wisely, as it turned out. He could not bear the thought of resuming work that had so exhausted him. His eyes, he said humorously, had looked upward for so long that he could not lower them to read a book or paper in the ordinary way, but had to lift it above his head, a disability that he claimed lasted quite a while. He used as an excuse to the pope that it was too much trouble to set up the scaffolding again.

"You ought at least to touch it up with gold," said the pope.

"Holy Father," said Michelangelo, "in those days men did not bedeck themselves in gold, and those you see there were never very rich. They were holy men who despised riches."

Pope Julius stopped pestering him after that sly rebuke, and began thinking again of the tomb he had ordered and which all too soon might enclose him.

After a short visit to Florence, Michelangelo returned to Rome in January, 1513, and began negotiations for the house in which he was to live for the remainder of his days when he was in Rome. This large dwelling in the Marcello de' Corvi ("Ravens' Lane") was at the western end of the Forum of Trajan, near the Church of Santa Maria di Loreto, opposite the present Vittorio Emanuele Monument. It has long since disappeared, but from a contract it is known to have had "several stories, reception rooms, bedrooms, grounds, a vegetable garden, wells, and other buildings." The last included two cottages. The Della Rovere family purchased this house for Michelangelo, but he had to pay rent on it until it was deeded to him in 1516. Here he moved the marbles which had been lying about the Piazza di San Pietro since 1505, and began to work on the figures for the tomb of Julius II, which the pope now wished to have erected in the Sistine Chapel.

Then, early in the morning of February 21, 1513, Pope Julius II died. Whatever his faults, and however great some historians consider them to have been, he was beloved of his people. At his funeral the guards were overpowered by the weeping crowds insisting on kissing the feet of the embalmed corpse. He was buried, however, not in the grandiose mausoleum he had ordered, but beside his uncle, Pope Sixtus IV, in the Capella del Santo Sacramento (Chapel of the Holy Sacrament) in St. Peter's.

If the death of his lavish but difficult patron affected Michelangelo emotionally, he made no mention of his grief in his letters. The financial problems of his family had vexed him all during his work in the Sistine Chapel, and he was still concerned with their health and welfare. Probably his immediate concern was with his own financial and artistic future in Rome, for he had no assurance that payments for his work on the tomb of Julius II would continue, or that the next pope would want his services.

Michelangelo had earned a great deal of money in Rome—enough to buy two pieces of farm property in Settignano and a house in Florence, and to set his brother Buonarroto up in the wool business. This accumulation of capital amounted almost to a passion with him. Doubtless he feared any loss of independence in thought and action, such as had made his father pitiable. Apparently even taking a wife and raising a family seemed a restriction on his freedom. "I have too much of a wife," he said to Vasari, "and that is this art . . . and my children will be the works I leave behind."

This slavery to economy, of course, restricted Michelangelo as much as improvidence might have done. He had no intention of turning his new house into a sort of club for courtiers as the young and equally successful Raphael was doing with his establishment in Rome. Instead, Michelangelo led a rather solitary life, except for the frequent dinner parties he went to in the houses of his friends of Florentine origin. The conclusion is inescapable that he was something of a sponger in this respect, yet the suspicion that anyone was sponging on him made him furious.

Such parties distracted Michelangelo from his own worries and from the agony of releasing his stupendous intellectual concepts into a form that might come somewhere near expressing what was in his mind. He could be amusing to others, and he liked anyone who amused him. He could also be quite a tease; he would encourage any pretentiousness he discovered in an inferior artist, then go into fits of laughter when the poor fellow was exposed. He loved to laugh even more at such a hack exposing himself. Then, after a spell, Michelangelo would grow tired of gossip and pranks, and retire to solitude.

Michelangelo's insecurity may have been due to his constant disappointment at finding a gap between what he wanted to express—and had to express in order to relieve his tensions—and what he was prevented from expressing either by persons or politics or the ultimate inability to make his hand the complete servant of his inner eye. His insecurity was probably also due to his basically simple nature and simple morality. The rivalries, the intrigues, and the feuds of Roman society baffled him and offended the principles which the doom-laden voice of Savonarola had long ago terrified him into accepting. As a result, Michelangelo grew suspicious and almost cynical in his distrust of other people's motives. The gigantic scope of his mind made it hard enough for him to live among pygmy intellects; it was even harder for a person of his strict morality to live in what he thought was an immoral society; and harder yet to have to struggle and suffer while watching the facile Raphael achieve an easier recognition. Pope Leo X made Raphael architect-in-chief of St. Peter's after Bramante's death in 1514. The young Umbrian painter thus became the arbiter of pontifical art.

Of Rome Michelangelo wrote bitterly:

> They make a sword or helmet from a chalice,
> And sell the blood of Christ here by the load,
> And cross and thorn become a shield, a blade,
> And even Christ is stripped of patience.
> —tr. Creighton Gilbert

Michelangelo's period of uncertainty at this time fortunately was brief. On March 11, 1513, the conclave of cardinals chose Giovanni de' Medici the next "Ruler of the World."

This nearsighted, thirty-eight-year-old son of Lorenzo the Magnificent, who had been an abbot since the age of seven and a cardinal since the age of thirteen, was thereafter to be known as Pope Leo X. His first recorded remark as the successor of St. Peter was made to his cousin: "Come, Giulio, let us enjoy the Papacy, since God has given it to Us." Then he gave the illegitimate Giulio de' Medici the cardinalate he himself had just vacated.

It took the pleasure-loving, frivolous, sensual Leo X longer to reward the puritanical, sardonic, ascetic artist who had made the previous pontificate more everlastingly celebrated by decorating the Sistine Chapel than Julius II had made it by all his short-lived conquests. Of the two rival geniuses, Leo preferred Raphael, whom he found more congenial and less demanding than Michelangelo.

The Della Rovere heirs of Julius II, and the executors of his will, took advantage of the new pope's delay. Julius' will provided for a huge outlay of money on the completion of his tomb. On May 6, 1513, the heirs and executors entered into a new contract with Michelangelo, according to which the sculptor was to complete the monument within seven years and meanwhile to undertake no other work that might interfere with that project.

Michelangelo thereupon went to work on the colossal figures for the tomb, which now was to be somewhat smaller than originally planned, and free-standing only on three sides. The new contract specified that there were to be forty statues.

The first of these Michelangelo completed was *The Rebellious Slave*, as it is now called, which is in the Louvre in Paris. It was finished, insofar as possible before being set into the tomb structure itself, by 1514. This marble nude, eight feet in height, was one of the twelve "slaves" intended for the lowest tier of the monument. They were probably designed to symbolize the provinces that Julius II had added to the papal states.

The powerfully muscled body of *The Rebellious Slave*, whose arms are bound behind his back, writhes to be free. The

The Rebellious Slave (Louvre, Paris)

tormented face is highly individualized and intensely dramatic. Strong contrasts of movement give the figure a dynamic quality that is almost unpleasant in its violence.

The Rebellious Slave is so closely related to the *St. Matthew* that it seems as if the years of work on the Sistine Chapel had been no interruption at all in the development of Michelangelo as a sculptor. Yet his experience as a painter definitely influenced his design of the statue. In *The Rebellious Slave* he is striving toward a well-outlined profile like that he had achieved in the decorative nudes he painted on the ceiling.

The effect of painting appears even more strongly in *The Dying Slave,* which Michelangelo was working on at approximately the same time as *The Rebellious Slave*. This marble nude, also in the Louvre, shows an even stronger influence on Michelangelo—that of the *Laocoön* group. It is practically a mirror image of the younger son (the one on the spectator's left) in that ancient group. The resemblance is so clear that the death struggle of Laocoön's son led to the title of Michelangelo's statue. But his slave is not dying; he is merely stirring in a deep sleep, as if he were dreaming of freedom.

The Dying Slave is thus a marvelous example of Michelangelo's transforming imagination. Its soft, lyrical quality is vastly different from the thundering drama of *The Rebellious Slave*. The lithe, sinuous lines of the youth's body have caused it often to be called Michelangelo's most beautiful statue. The young man is so wholly abandoned to the joy of his dream of freedom that the spectator hardly notices the band across his chest that binds him.

The influence of the *Laocoön* is also strong on Michelangelo's conception of his *Moses,* work on which commenced about the end of August, 1514. Michelangelo was, of course, working with at least three assistants in his house in the Macello de' Corvi; these helpers blocked out the statues accord-

The Dying Slave (Louvre, Paris)

ing to his designs, and also worked out the purely decorative elements of the tomb. The *Moses* was finished in 1516.

The nearly seven-foot-high *Moses* is the only one of the statues originally planned for the tomb that is now on the tomb. Coming at the end of Michelangelo's second great period of sculpture, it stands in dramatic contrast to his work at the end of his first period of maturity. The *David* of that period, also colossal in size, speaks of calm, balanced nobility of thought. The *Moses* is the sheer dynamic power of thought. As Condivi said of it, the figure is a "wise, tired, and sorrowful thinker, whose countenance inspires both love and awe."

The action of the *Moses* is not imminent, as in the *David;* instead the figure of the prophet and leader, absorbed in thought, demonstrates that thought is action. The mighty marble figure is Michelangelo's projection into three-dimensional form of the mind of God which he depicted in the swirling figure of the Creator on the ceiling of the Sistine Chapel.

Moses was intended for the second tier of the tomb; that is, the statue was designed to be seen from below. Its present position at floor level, therefore, makes it seem out of proportion. Consequently, the *terribilità* implicit in the figure has been somewhat lost; it has to be imagined rather than literally seen. Photographs make this sublime, awesome quality more real than the statue itself does. Study, for example, how the light flickers in a spiral along the folds of the robe, on the delicately modeled strong fingers, on the ripples of the beard. The spiral of light winds through the swirling locks and ends in the horns*

* The horns are due to a mistranslation in the Vulgate (Latin version of the Scriptures) of the Hebrew word for "rays of light." Michelangelo was aware of this error, but kept the horns to symbolize the light that shone from Moses' brow. It was obviously impossible for him to represent the rays in three-dimensional stone.

Moses (San Pietro in Vincoli, Rome)

atop the forehead. The result is that the titanic figure quivers with energy as if the living prophet were receiving from Jehovah a message beyond that contained in the tables of the law which Moses holds almost casually.

By June of 1515, Pope Leo X had quarreled with Francesco Maria della Rovere, Duke of Urbino, and nephew of the late Pope Julius II. The duke refused to support the pope against the French. It then became clear to Michelangelo that Pope Leo would try to get the sculptor into his own service if for no other reason than to break off his work on the Della Rovere tomb.

Michelangelo speeded up his work on the *Moses*, for he had no wish to be interrupted again in the project that meant so much to him. His fears were well grounded, for, in March, 1516, Pope Leo X excommunicated the uncooperative Duke of Urbino, and gave his lands and title to his own nephew, Lorenzo de' Medici, the son of the Piero de' Medici who had been exiled from Florence in 1494.

In the meantime Pope Leo had paid a long visit to his native Florence. As Cardinal Giovanni de' Medici he had supported Pope Julius II against the Florentines, who were allied with the French, whom the papal forces had forced to retire to Milan. As a result, Cardinal Giovanni de' Medici had got the "lifetime" Gonfalonier Piero Soderini exiled from Florence and the Medici family restored to power in that city. He himself became the virtual ruler of Florence. After he was elected pope, he made the city an annex of the papacy. Pope Leo then gave the administration of Florence to his brother Giuliano, who, by marriage to a French princess, became Duke of Nemours.

The Florentines, who had gone wild with joy over the election of one of their citizens to the papacy, welcomed Pope Leo X to the city with gorgeous pageantry. It was probably during his three months' stay in Florence that Pope Leo decided to make the Medici family's parish church of San Lorenzo (St.

Lawrence) into a shrine worthy of his exalted self and of his
illustrious forebears. Perhaps the decision entered his mind as
he sang mass in the church shortly after his arrival on November 30, 1515, and wept as he prayed before the tomb of his
father, Lorenzo the Magnificent.

Leo X did not return to Rome until February 20, 1516. A
month later Giuliano de' Medici, Duke of Nemours, died in
Florence, and was succeeded by his nephew Lorenzo, shortly to
be named Duke of Urbino.

Pope Leo announced a competition for designs for the decoration of the Church of San Lorenzo. Its architect, Filippo
Brunelleschi, had left it, in 1446, without a finished facade at
the east end—a rather common practice of fifteenth-century
Italian architects who had not yet found a solution for designing a facade that would be in the new classical style and would
still conform to the traditional (nave and side aisle) design of
the interior of the church.

The pope invited several architects to submit plans for a new
facade for San Lorenzo, and he determined to engage Michelangelo to do the sculpture for it. Leo envisioned the facade as
merely a framework for statues and reliefs. He had probably got
the idea from the elaborate decorations on the Cathedral of
Florence at the time of his magnificent welcome from the city.

In order to get Michelangelo's services, Pope Leo forced the
Della Rovere heirs to release the sculptor from work on the
tomb of Julius II. Consequently, Michelangelo, on July 8, 1516,
made a new contract with them. This extended the date of
completion of the tomb to nine years, permitted him to work on
the statues—now reduced to twenty-three—wherever he
pleased, and again diminished the dimensions of the entire
structure. Shortly after this contract was signed, Michelangelo
left Rome for a visit to Florence, and then went to Carrara to
get more marble quarried for the tomb.

By October 7, 1516, the pope seems to have made up his mind to give the entire work—architecture and sculpture—of the facade of San Lorenzo to Michelangelo. While he was still in Carrara, Michelangelo learned of this decision through letters from a friend. He was violently angry. He stayed in Carrara, where he had rented a house soon after his arrival there in September, until Pope Leo summoned him to the Vatican. Only then, on December 5, 1516, did Michelangelo leave Carrara for Rome.

After Michelangelo met with the pope, the pontiff ordered him to make a design for the facade of San Lorenzo. He may have had to do it on the spot; certainly within a few days. At any rate, he was trapped. He did not dare produce an inferior design, even if his artistic integrity had permitted him to.

When Michelangelo showed the pope the design he had made, Leo declared that he liked it the best of all the submissions. The pope immediately directed him to return to Carrara to quarry marble for the facade.

Michelangelo protested that he was bound to the Della Rovere heirs by contract.

"Leave me to deal with them," said the pope. "I will content them."

Leo X sent for the heirs and forced them to release Michelangelo. They wept. Michelangelo wept. The best he could do was to get the pope to promise to ship the marbles for the tomb to Florence at the papal expense, so that Michelangelo could work on them there while also engaged on the facade of San Lorenzo.

Disconsolately Michelangelo left Rome for Carrara again on December 31, 1516.*

* Although the above account of this confused episode is plausible and is well-evidenced, it should be admitted that there also is evidence that (1) the Della Rovere heirs, having fallen on hard times, were rather

Michelangelo seems to have been overconfident. Although he had protested to Pope Julius II that he was a sculptor, not a painter, he had nonetheless produced the masterpiece of the Sistine Chapel ceiling. What he had learned from that long painting experience he had adapted into sculpture, and had produced such masterpieces as *The Dying Slave* and the *Moses*. Apparently he believed that although he had had little practice in architecture, he could be as eminent in that field of art as he had proved to be in painting and sculpture.

"I feel myself qualified," Michelangelo wrote to an architect in Rome on May 2, 1517, "to execute the project of the facade of San Lorenzo in such a manner that it will be, both architecturally and sculpturally, the mirror of all Italy."

He was wrong. None of the several designs and models he made for the facade before a contract for the work was signed on January 19, 1518, shows any notable originality. In fact, the final design, and particularly the final model, are stiff and dry. (The addition of sculptures and reliefs, however, might have remedied this unattractive quality of the design.) Michelangelo was clearly not ready for so complicated an architectural project.

Furthermore, Michelangelo insisted on working alone and in secret. Pope Leo had appointed co-workers and assistants; Michelangelo got rid of them and demanded sole authority. This independence of his naturally stirred up considerable antagonism among the artists in Rome who wanted some share in the monument the pope was planning. They intrigued and conspired against Michelangelo.

---

willing to negotiate a new contract and may have initiated it; (2) that Michelangelo had made some effort to get the commission for the facade and its sculpture; (3) that having thus found himself more involved in both projects (tomb and facade) than he wished to be, he tried hard to get out of the trap; (4) that Pope Leo, having got Michelangelo's services at last, had no intention of releasing him. The key documents in the case are missing.

Owing to his work in Carrara and Florence, Michelangelo could seldom be in Rome to protect himself, even if he had had the ability in counterintrigue to do so. As a result, Pope Leo lost a great deal of his interest in the project; his cousin, Cardinal Giulio de' Medici, was more in sympathy with Michelangelo's dedication to his art and with the memorial to the Medici family. Cardinal Giulio had succeeded to the rule of Florence after the death of Lorenzo, Duke of Urbino, on May 4, 1519.

These intrigues may have led to the horrendous difficulties Michelangelo encountered in quarrying the marble for the facade of San Lorenzo. Florence had just acquired the rights to quarry marble in the commune of Seravezza, which included the southern two mountains of the Carrara range. Word got to Pope Leo that the marble in that section of the mountains was better than that in the Carrara section. Furthermore, the Seravezza marble would bring revenue to Medici-controlled Florence, instead of to the Marquis of Carrara. The pope, therefore, commanded Michelangelo to open up the marble veins of the Florentine territory, even though Michelangelo considered the marble of Seravezza unsuitable. Also, he would have to build a road several miles long from the mountains to the sea in order to get the marble out and to Florence. Naturally, the Carrarese were furious, and accused Michelangelo of dishonesty. Therefore, he lost the cooperation of the quarry workers with whom he had had good dealings since 1498.

Then, on March 10, 1520, Pope Leo X canceled the contract for the facade of San Lorenzo. The reasons for this termination are hard to discover. Undoubtedly Michelangelo's irritability had a great deal to do with it. He knew he was wasting time— something he abhorred—on the unnecessary and difficult task of getting the marble out of the Seravezza quarries. The workmen he had to employ there were inexperienced and unreliable. Cardinal Giulio appropriated to his own projects some of the

marble Michelangelo had extracted for San Lorenzo. The
whole affair was insulting to Michelangelo as a man and as an
artist. He can scarcely be blamed for letting it inflame his never
very cool temper.

On the other hand, it is fairly clear that Michelangelo's
enemies in Rome had considerable to do with Pope Leo's
unjustifiable cancellation of the contract. At least one of these
foes, Cardinal Giulio's secretary, Domenico Buoninsegni, tried
to get Michelangelo to join him in making a profit out of the
project of the facade. When Michelangelo refused to be a party
to such dishonesty, his enemy, says Vasari, "was so enraged that
he employed every means to humiliate and injure Michelangelo, though he acted covertly."

At any rate, the physical and intellectual energies that Michelangelo had given to the project for more than three years
were wasted. The facade of San Lorenzo is still as rough and
unornamented today as it was before Pope Leo conceived its
redecoration in 1515–16. The only benefit to the bitterly disappointed Michelangelo was the experience in engineering he
got from having to open up the Seravezza quarries and build
the road through the hills and over the marshes for transporting
their products.

VIII: THOUGHT AND ACTION

The years during which Michelangelo was principally occupied with the abortive project of the facade of San Lorenzo were not an entire waste of time for him. By the summer of 1519, he had begun four more statues of slaves for the tomb of Julius II, and was at work on the second version of a statue of Christ.

This statue had been commissioned on June 14, 1514, by four Roman gentlemen, and Michelangelo had begun a previous version, only to find a black vein inside the marble block which forced him to abandon it. He started the second version, now in the Church of Santa Maria sopra Minerva (that is, built above the remains of a temple of Minerva), Rome, toward the end of 1518. By April 20, 1520, Michelangelo was ready to ship it from Florence to Rome, but difficulties about the payments for it kept him from doing so for another year.

Michelangelo sent his assistant Piero Urbano to Rome to put the finishing touches on the statue after it had been installed in a poorly lighted spot of the dim Gothic church. Urbano did a great deal of damage to the right foot, to the hands, and to the beard of the figure; but another Florentine sculptor, Federigo Frizzi, managed somewhat to repair this. The statue was unveiled on December 27, 1521.

142

Of all the major works of Michelangelo, this *Christ* is the least appealing. Even Michelangelo was dissatisfied with it, and offered to do another version. But his patrons were pleased enough with the imperfect one they had at last received.

The six-and-a-half-foot-high marble figure is totally nude. (A bronze drapery, added later, is distracting; even more so is a bronze sandal added to conceal the damage Urbano did to the foot.) This concept of Christ is quite in accordance with Church tradition and was intended to represent the complete humiliation of the Savior during His torture by the Roman soldiers and His crucifixion. Indeed, the contract for the work specified "a nude Christ." Consequently, Michelangelo executed the *Christ* as he might a pagan deity like the *Bacchus,* or an Old Testament hero, or an allegorical figure. It is simply an unsuitable treatment for the supreme hero of Christianity. In the equally nude Christ of the *Crucifix of Santo Spirito* (page 35), the treatment is much more in keeping with the subject.

The instruments of suffering which Christ holds here—cross, sponge, reed—are unusual ones. Missing are the more traditional crown of thorns and the wounds, especially the wound in the side. Hence, there is little indication of Christ's shedding of His blood for the remission of sins. The dramatic gesture of the right hand reaching across the body to point at the bizarre symbols, however, indicates that Michelangelo attached a special significance to them. He may have intended the statue as a symbol of man's sacrifice for man, but it remains too literal a statement to arouse the emotional response due that subject.

The four slaves, now in the Academy of Fine Arts in Florence, were never completed. They are known as *The Young Slave, The Bearded Slave, The Awakening Slave,* and *The Atlas Slave.* Like the *St. Matthew* they are only sketches, but the modeling of their powerful nude bodies makes them very

Christ (Santa Maria sopra Minerva, Rome)

The Four Slaves (Academy of Fine Arts, Florence)

a. *The Young Slave*

b. *The Bearded Slave*

c. *The Awakening Slave*

d. *The Atlas Slave*

much alive. They seem to struggle on their own account to be free of the stone that imprisons them. In contrast with the all too finished *Christ,* the four unfinished slaves are an eloquent and unequivocal expression of Michelangelo's thinking about the relationship of form and matter.

Perhaps to this period also belongs the splendid *Victory,* now in the Palazzo Vecchio, Florence. It was intended for the tomb of Julius II, but its style is close to that of the sculptures for the Medici Chapel, which Michelangelo was about to commence; hence, it may have been as late as 1534 when those sculptures were ended. Unlike the four Slaves, the *Victory* is almost finished.

The eight-and-a-half-foot-high marble nude youth kneels on a roughly finished giant. His beautiful body is surmounted by a remarkably handsome head with curly hair (symbolizing victory) and flashing eyes. The drama of the figure lies in the typically Michelangelesque gesture of the right arm casually reaching up to adjust a cloak that hangs from the right shoulder. The left arm reaches behind the body for a sword with which to decapitate the giant. The smooth, muscled body twists, as the youth presses his left leg on his fallen foe, so gracefully that he seems almost indifferent to his triumph. This casual grace and lyrical rhythm contrast vividly with the tension of the pose and with the toadlike, hunched posture of the aged giant. In its own way the *Victory* is as appealing as the *Pietà* and as the great *David.*

Michelangelo had made Florence his headquarters for his work on the facade of San Lorenzo, even though he spent much of the three years he was engaged with it in the Seravezza district. On July 14, 1518, he had bought property in Florence on the Via Mozza (now the Via San Zenoni), and added another lot to it on November 24. Here, near San Lorenzo, he erected a workshop that would accommodate twenty figures at a

Victory (Palazzo Vecchio, Florence)

time, and a shed to protect the marbles he had had shipped from Rome and those he would acquire from Seravezza.

Michelangelo, however, lived in his house on the Via Ghibellina, in the diagonally opposite section of Florence, presumably with his father. The old man now took great delight in the meaningless title of "count," which he had received from the pope as the crown of his meaningless life. Buonarroto was married, for the second time. Giovan Simone, whose fecklessness had driven Michelangelo into a fury, had settled down into an uneventful life, and, as he was unmarried, probably lived with his father also. Sigismondo was a farmer in Settignano, an occupation Michelangelo considered undignified for one of his family. By remaining in Florence, Michelangelo could at least keep an eye on these dependents of his, and they were pleased to have their principal source of supply so close at hand.

Michelangelo, therefore, was happy to remain in Florence in spite of the cancellation of the contract. He made no effort to conciliate Pope Leo X, or to return to Rome.

The pope had no true dislike of Michelangelo, and apparently wished him to return to Rome. Perhaps he felt guilty over having wasted Michelangelo's efforts on a project that he had only halfheartedly supported. The two men, of almost exactly the same age, had been friends since the time of their adolescence, when Michelangelo lived in the Medici household. A friend of Michelangelo, the distinguished painter Sebastiano del Piombo, wrote him that when the pope "speaks of you, it would seem that he were talking about a brother, almost with tears in his eyes."

Sebastiano, however, added: "But you frighten everybody, even popes!" And the dauntless Pope Julius II had remarked of Michelangelo: "He is terrible. No one can get on with him."

Pope Leo and Cardinal Giulio de' Medici, therefore, were not long in finding another project for Michelangelo. By November, 1520, they had discussed with him their plan for erecting in the new sacristy of the Church of San Lorenzo monuments over the tombs of their recently deceased relatives: Giuliano de' Medici, Duke of Nemours; and Lorenzo de' Medici, Duke of Urbino.

The construction of this new sacristy—really a burial chapel —on the east side of the south transept of San Lorenzo had been renewed in March, 1520, after a long lapse. It was to have been a duplicate of Brunelleschi's "old" sacristy on the north transept, but Michelangelo was to be permitted to change that design.

The necessity of such a change soon was apparent if the sacristy was to contain an altar, two wall tombs for the dukes, a double wall tomb for Lorenzo the Magnificent and his brother, and free-standing tombs for Pope Leo X and Cardinal Giulio de' Medici. The several drawings Michelangelo made for the accommodation of these monuments indicate that he may have had many conferences with the Medici before the more-or-less final design was approved in March, 1521. By April 9 of that year Michelangelo had received money for the first marble he would need for the monuments. He then went to the Pietra Santa quarry in the Seravezza region to superintend the cutting of the stones.

Michelangelo had before him the splendid example of Brunelleschi's sacristy, but this was in the conservative classical style of the previous century. Michelangelo retained enough of this rigidly proportioned, dignified style to serve as contrast to his innovations. The chief departure he made from the former style was to use architectural members—pillars, pilasters, pediments, and cornices—for ornamental rather than functional purposes. His approach was that of a sculptor rather than of an architect.

Given a partially completed building, and being artistically

The Medici Chapel (San Lorenzo, Florence)

obliged to keep it harmonious with Brunelleschi's sacristy, Michelangelo faced a considerable architectural problem. The crux of this problem lay in the tradition of framing a wall tomb in a niche. The niche symbolized the elevation of a deceased ruler into Heaven, where he would become a divinity—like the deified Roman emperors. Michelangelo recognized that the construction of nonfunctional niches for the tombs would rob the new sacristy of the impressive sense of space that Brunelleschi had achieved in the old sacristy. It was at least five years before Michelangelo found an adequate, if not entirely satisfactory, solution for the problem.

His answer is a blend of function and decoration into a fantasy. The sacristy becomes a half-real, half-imaginary little world of its own. Its charm lies in the rhythm Michelangelo invented for the functional and the purely ornamental elements. Both these elements seem to belong to a well-articulated anatomy. The building, in that sense, is like Michelangelo's *Moses*, in which the prophet's flowing robe and the tablets he holds (ornament) are as much a part of the total figure as his actual body (function).

While the solution of this architectural problem was developing in Michelangelo's mind, he was at work on the tombs themselves. As these monuments progressed, Michelangelo's ideas for the architecture changed. The sequence of the changes reflects not only the relentless logic of Michelangelo's thinking, but also his capacity to adjust to circumstances beyond his control. The discouraging experience of the fruitless project of the facade of San Lorenzo had matured him. He was not becoming a placid person—his single-minded and passionate devotion to his art was too great for that—but he was learning at least to cooperate with the inevitable.

The "inevitable" expressed itself in the death, on December 1, 1521, of Pope Leo X. In spite of Cardinal Giulio de' Medici's machinations to get the conclave to elect a successor favorable to his family, their choice went to Cardinal Adrian Dedel of Utrecht. The new pope, Adrian VI, had no interest whatever in any of the arts that his two predecessors had so enthusiastically patronized. It is said that he proposed the obliteration of Michelangelo's Sistine Chapel ceiling on the grounds that those superb frescoes were indecent.

Pope Adrian, who had no love for the Medici, quickly confirmed the rights of the Della Rovere family to their duchy of Urbino, which Leo X had appropriated. Since the pope could see no reason why Michelangelo should work on tombs for the Medici family, he urged the Della Roveres to put pressure on the sculptor to fulfill his contract to them for the tomb of Julius II. As soon as the 1516 contract for the tomb expired, on May 6, 1522, the heirs of Pope Julius did so.

Michelangelo appears to have been eager to honor his obligations to the Della Roveres, if for no other reason than that the tomb would be such a splendid display of his genius. On the other hand, Cardinal Giulio de' Medici, who had discreetly retired to Florence, which he proceeded to rule with considerable justice and efficiency, put an equal amount of pressure on Michelangelo to work on the Medici tombs.

Michelangelo seems to have played it safe, and to have worked on the figures for the tomb of Julius II—presumably on the four slaves that he had begun earlier (pp. 144–7). The blocking out of these figures had been done, under Michelangelo's direction, by his assistants, but the emerging forms themselves show the touch of his own hand.

The reactionary Pope Adrian VI died on September 14, 1523. On November 19, Cardinal Giulio de' Medici was elected to succeed him as Pope Clement VII.

The new pope immediately settled the squabble with the Della Roveres so diplomatically that they virtually went over to

Michelangelo's side. Michelangelo had been ready to repay the money the Della Roveres had given him, but a compromise was reached whereby he would again reduce the size of the project and prepare a simple wall tomb as a monument to Pope Julius II.

Largely owing to the preoccupation of Pope Leo X with the extraordinary complications with which he had involved the papacy, his cousin, while still Cardinal Giulio, had been the principal negotiator with Michelangelo for the new sacristy of San Lorenzo. Now that Giulio was not only head of the Medici family but the unopposed ruler of Florence, and pope as well, he firmly directed Michelangelo to devote all his energies to the sacristy, now known as the Medici Chapel. In addition, by January, 1524, Clement VII directed Michelangelo to prepare designs for a library the pope intended to build in Florence to house the famous collection of Medici books and manuscripts.

Michelangelo was deeply disappointed over this turn of affairs. His heart was more in his work on the tomb of Julius II than on the Medici Chapel. To renege on the Della Rovere tomb also seemed dishonest to him, and he knew that he was being gossiped about as an impostor and opportunist for not completing the tomb and for switching his allegiance. For ten months he refused the generous monthly salary and the house the pope had offered him. He was too distracted to work on either project.

Finally Michelangelo's friends prevailed on him to accept the pope's commissions. Michelangelo then drew his back salary, and moved into the house—Casa de Macciagnini, near San Lorenzo—in October, 1524. This decision, as Michelangelo wrote to his financial agent in Rome, would at least make him appear "like a man of honor" and squelch the gossip. But he was heartbroken over having to give up the tomb of Julius II again.

For the next ten years Michelangelo labored on the completion of the Medici Chapel itself, on the tombs of the Medici family, and on the Medici Library (called the Laurentian Library because of its situation; it adjoins the north side of the nave of the Church of San Lorenzo, fitting into the corner formed by the north transept). There were frequent changes in the plans for all of these projects; Pope Clement kept thinking up additional projects; and there were the interruptions of the "inevitable."

One of Clement's additional projects, announced in October, 1525, was a colossal statue to be built from marble blocks and erected on the Piazza di San Lorenzo, facing the Medici palace. Michelangelo, however, quickly disposed of this bizarre idea by ridiculing it.

Then all Michelangelo's work on the Medici projects stopped as a result of Clement VII's disastrous embroilments with the Holy Roman Emperor Charles V. These culminated in the terrible sack of Rome by Charles's army, which began its desecration of the city on May 6, 1527. The pope took refuge in the Castel Sant' Angelo, where Charles V kept him a prisoner until the end of the year.

The result of this outrage was a rebellion of the Florentines against their Medici rulers. On May 17, they drove Clement's representative out of their city along with the two young Medici princes in his charge. On May 31, the Florentines reestablished a republic with Niccolò Capponi as gonfalonier.

The new government offered Michelangelo a minor appointment as clerk to a commission that handled affairs in Florentine territory outside the city proper, but he did not think it worth accepting. Apparently he had little respect for Capponi's middle-of-the-road administration, which certainly seems to have lacked intelligent discipline and to have failed to inspire confidence in the citizens.

The Florentines lived in fear of reprisal from the pope on the one hand, and of attacks from Charles V on the other hand. As if to increase their anxiety, plague broke out in the city in August, 1527. It is said, probably with some exaggeration, to have wiped out thirty thousand lives, one third of the population! One of its victims was Michelangelo's brother Buonarroto, who succumbed on July 2, 1528. His death placed the burden of his family on the grieving Michelangelo, who repaid the widow's dowry, placed Buonarroto's daughter in a convent at his own expense, and undertook the expenses of his young nephew Lionardo, who went to live with his grandfather.

By that time, Emperor Charles V had released Pope Clement VII, who escaped from Rome to Orvieto. In anticipation of the pope's revenge on the city that had rebelled against him and his family, the war department of the Florentine republic appointed Michelangelo director of the city fortifications on April 6, 1529.

For some time previous to this official appointment, Michelangelo had been engaged in erecting defense works in the city. Now he immediately devoted his efforts to fortifying the hill of San Miniato, on the south bank of the Arno, from which an enemy could control the city.

On June 29, 1529, the danger to Florence ceased to be a fear and became a fact, for the emperor and the pope then came to an agreement whereby Florence was handed over to the vengeance of Clement VII. A month later Michelangelo made a visit to Ferrara to inspect its famous fortifications. On his return he found that Niccolò Capponi had had the fortifications of San Miniato dismantled.

The discovery made it clear to Michelangelo that there was a plot against him in the war department, and that Gonfalonier Capponi was listening more to the foreign general whom the department had hired, Malatesta Baglioni, than to one of its own citizens. Michelangelo distrusted that mercenary soldier. He was well aware that the anti-Medicean party had opposed his appointment on the logical ground that he had been employed by Clement VII. His terror of physical damage to himself returned. One night he was warned that his fear was justified. Michelangelo fled for safety to Venice on September 21. On September 30, the Florentine government declared him an outlaw.

Michelangelo's friends in Florence, however, begged him to return. About October 10, after he was reasonably sure that the danger to himself was past, and he had received a safe-conduct, he resolved to return. He did not reach Florence, however, until about November 20, owing to the illness of his traveling companions and to the roundabout route he had to take. For Pope Clement's army had begun its siege of Florence on October 10, 1529.

Forgiven by the signoria, who preferred to have his services than to punish him, Michelangelo immediately began refortifying San Miniato.

Michelangelo's considerable contribution to the art of defensive architecture was due to his appreciation of the fact that the greatly increased use of heavy, mobile artillery in warfare had rendered old styles of fortification obsolete. He also saw that fortifications must now serve for offense as well as defense. Hence, he concentrated on giving the defenders room to move about inside the fortifications, and many projecting points from which to attack besiegers. The result was designs for walls and bastions like gigantic claws—a dynamic kind of construction intended to bring the protected defenders literally into the midst of the attackers instead of leaving the defenders static and relatively passive.

Unfortunately Michelangelo overlooked the fact that cannonballs would be descending into these claws as well as be

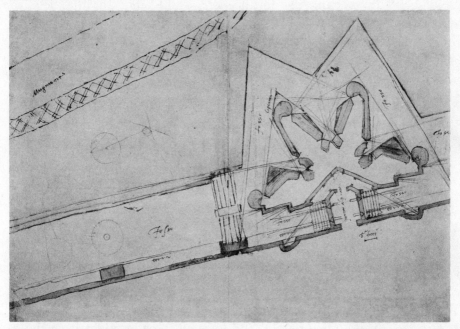
Michelangelo's drawing for a fortification

projected from them. Later he learned to correct blind spots which could not be covered by protective fire from other positions and so actually gave cover to an enemy close to them.

In erecting the fortifications of Florence for the siege of 1529–30, Michelangelo went about the work, it is said, "with lasting and diligent effort, freely and lovingly." He was eager to make himself as useful as possible in the serious situation, but he did not have time fully to execute the designs he had made. His temporary expedient was to build walls and salients of earth and straw and unbaked brick. These absorbed the shock of enemy missiles.

The most ingenious of Michelangelo's hurriedly erected defenses of San Miniato was his scheme to protect the bell tower of the church, obviously a great vantage point. It already had been seriously damaged by enemy fire, and there was danger that it would crash down upon the soldiers in the bastion beneath it. Michelangelo, says Condivi,

> . . . caused a large number of mattresses well stuffed with wool to be brought, and lowered these by night from the summit of the tower down to its foundations, protecting those parts that were exposed to fire. Inasmuch as the cornice projected, the mattresses hung free in the air, at the distance of six cubits from the wall; so that when the missiles of the enemy arrived, they did little or no damage, partly owing to the distance they had traveled, and partly to the resistance offered by this swinging, yielding panoply.

The tower survived the siege. It was fully rebuilt about 1550. Florence, however, was already doomed. For eight months the death agony went on. Then, in August, betrayed by Malatesta Baglioni, the city surrendered. The capitulation was signed on August 12, 1530, and the Medici were reinstated.

Pope Clement took a fearful revenge on the patriots of the Florentine republic, which had been extinguished forever. Anticipating that this vengeance would light on him, Michelangelo went into hiding in the bell tower of the Church of San Niccolò on the south side of the Arno. Clement's wrath cooled down, however, and he gave orders that when Michelangelo was found, he should be treated with courtesy.

Michelangelo then emerged from hiding and went to Rome to make his peace with the pope. Clement forgave him, and sent him back to Florence with orders to finish the library and the Medici Chapel. But the pope threatened to excommunicate him if he undertook any other work except what he was obliged by contract to do for the heirs of Pope Julius II.

The eternal tomb continued, therefore, to be a psychological burden to Michelangelo as heavy as its blocks of marble themselves. Gossip that he had misused the funds given him for completing it troubled him. He saw his grandiose plan whittled away. A third contract, dated April 29, 1532, was financially unfavorable to Michelangelo, and reduced the design to a simple wall tomb which was to be completed in three years and placed in the Della Rovere family church, San Pietro in Vincoli, in Rome. Pope Clement permitted Michelangelo to spend four months of every year in Rome in order to supervise work on the tomb, some of which was to be executed by other hands than Michelangelo's own. He was to do only six statues himself.

Michelangelo returned unwillingly to Florence. The political atmosphere there was hostile to him. The pope's illegitimate son, Alessandro de' Medici, whom Clement had installed as ruler of Florence on May 1, 1532, was an unprincipled tyrant. He made existence humiliating for any liberty-loving Florentine, and his animosity toward Michelangelo in particular could easily have cost the artist his life if he had not been under the protection of the pope.

Michelangelo's old enemy, Buoninsegni, continued to conspire against him by supporting a rival sculptor, the utterly inept Baccio Bandinelli.

Bandinelli's father actually broke into Michelangelo's workshop, destroyed many of Michelangelo's designs, and damaged some marbles. This vandalism was designed to insure Baccio Bandinelli's getting the commission for a sculpture that the signoria wanted to erect opposite Michelangelo's *David* before their palace. As early as 1508 plans had been discussed with Michelangelo for executing such a group, and Michelangelo had made designs for it. Through intrigue, Bandinelli finally got the contract, but the statue (*Hercules Slaying Cacus*) that he produced has been for over four hundred years one of the most painful eyesores on public display.

Personal grief was added to Michelangelo's professional difficulties. His father, whom he dearly loved in spite of the old man's stupidity and ineptness, died at the age of eighty-six in the spring of 1531, probably as a result of privations caused by the siege of Florence. Lodovico Buonarroti's death occasioned some of Michelangelo's finest lines of poetry:

> The night decreases not your splendor,
> Nor does it brighter shine by day,
> However bright the sun that heats our frame.
>
> Dear father, from your dying, I learn to die.
> In thoughts I see you in that place
> Which earthly woes hide from our mortal eyes.
>
> Death therefore seems no harsh disgrace
> For one whose last day brings him to the God
> Whom he had left upon his first.

For, near God's throne I think you now
By grace, and there, I hope we'll meet, if reason can
Draw my cold heart above this earthly slime.

By the following year Michelangelo was comforted by the acquaintance he made on one of his many visits to Rome of Tommaso de' Cavalieri. They became mutually devoted friends, although Cavalieri was some thirty-four years younger than the artist. This charming, rich Roman nobleman had a fine collection of antique sculpture and of drawings, and was deeply interested in music. Music, in fact, may have brought him and Michelangelo together, for about this time several of Michelangelo's poems were being set to music by some of the best composers of the period. These songs, like the poems themselves, were "published" by being circulated in manuscript among the friends of the author or composer, then by them to their friends, and so on. Cavalieri was grateful for the friendship of so supremely gifted a man as Michelangelo, and the prickly Michelangelo softened noticeably under the influence of that graceful, untormented young man of distinction.

Michelangelo made three beautiful drawings for his "Tommao"—a *Ganymede,* a *Phaeton,* and a *Tityus*—all humanistic subjects from classical mythology. One of the few portraits he is known to have done was of this friend.

Michelangelo's drawings,* which date from his earliest essays in art to the time, some eighty years later, when his fingers

* Michelangelo's drawings are scattered throughout the museums of the world. The most outstanding collections are in the Casa Buonarroti and the Uffizi Gallery, Florence; the British Museum, London; the Albertina, Vienna; and the Louvre, Paris. Two are in the Metropolitan Museum of Art, New York City; and one is in the Institute of Fine Arts, Detroit.

Phaeton

were too stiff to hold a pen, are among his greatest achievements. Many are studies for paintings or statues. These he used as discipline of an idea until he became absolute master of it. Others, like those for Cavalieri, he regarded as complete in themselves. He simply chose the medium of pen and ink, or charcoal, or chalk, or a wash to express a certain idea. The latter are so exquisitely modeled and shaded that, in spite of their monotone, they suggest a multiplicity of colors. Often these, like the ones for Cavalieri, are intensely personal, for they were conceived as a gift to a private individual rather than for public display. Introspective and sensitive, they are, in a sense, Michelangelo's secret diary.

In spite of the prohibitions of Clement VII against Michelangelo's undertaking other work than the pope's and the Della Roveres', Michelangelo did at least two "unauthorized" pieces. One was a painting, *Leda and the Swan*, which he gave to the Duke of Ferrara out of gratitude for the duke's courtesy to him on his visit in 1529. This work has disappeared, and is known only through several copies of it. Obviously intended for the private amusement of the duke and his male friends, it was Michelangelo's only known excursion into the field of erotica. The figure of Leda, however, is similar to that of Michelangelo's marble *Night*, which he was probably working on at the same time for the Medici Chapel.

The other piece, executed for Baccio Valori, the pope's representative in Florence, was done at Valori's request as a compensation for Valori's protection of Michelangelo during the purge of patriots after the surrender of the city to the papal forces in 1530.

This small (forty inches high) *Apollo*, now in the Bargello in Florence, was altered from an unfinished *David* in Michelangelo's studio in order to gratify Valori's preference for classical subjects over biblical ones. The youthful nude figure is

Apollo (Bargello, Florence)

singularly soft and lyrical, almost effeminate. The dramatic gesture of the left arm reaching across the chest perhaps to draw an arrow from a quiver, and the rough finish of the marble of the figure's back, save it from the weakness that the otherwise languid, dreamy pose suggests. The mysterious harmony of the statue, produced by the vigorous gesture caught in a moment of suspension—a sort of incomplete completeness—makes it the most provocative of Michelangelo's minor pieces of sculpture.

These two works must have given Michelangelo some welcome diversion from his efforts to realize in plastic form his deep thinking on the somber subject of the roles of action and of thought in life and their connection with the factor of time. For such is the theme of the sculptures he conceived for the burial chapel of the Medici family in the Church of San Lorenzo.

Of the four monuments Michelangelo originally planned, he executed two—for Lorenzo de' Medici, Duke of Urbino, and for Giuliano de' Medici, Duke of Nemours. Each of these was to have consisted of several more figures than were eventually produced—two river gods at the base of each sarcophagus; two standing figures in the niches on either side of the central seated figures symbolizing thought and action. Only the latter exist, plus the four figures representing night and day, dawn and twilight, which recline on the sarcophagus lids.

A free-standing *Madonna*, flanked by figures of the patron saints of the Medici—*St. Cosmas* (by Giovanni Montorsorli) and *St. Damian* (by Raffaello da Montelupo)—stands on a low stone chest between the tombs of the dukes and opposite the simple altar. The chest contains the remains of Lorenzo the Magnificent and his murdered brother Giuliano.*

* The dating of the sculptures in the Medici Chapel is only vaguely documented. The probable dates are:

1521. *Madonna* begun. Brought to present state, 1534.

The tomb of Lorenzo is on the left of the single, low entrance to the chapel. In the architectural tabernacle above the sarcophagus sits a man in a helmet shaped as a lion's head. He wears the formfitting "leather" armor of the ancient Roman generals, which conforms to the shape and posture of his powerful body. He represents thought. His head, which rests on his left hand, is deeply bowed. The left elbow rests on a box decorated with a bat's mask, possibly symbolizing the way a thinking man preserves his treasure. The legs, crossed at the ankles, signify repose, but they are electric with concealed energy—the power of thought. The extended right arm, the wrist doubled back as it rests on the knee, is similarly passive, but the angles of the elbow and the wrist give it vitality.

The figure is no portrait of the duke. When blamed for not making it resemble the ruthless Lorenzo, Michelangelo tartly replied that a thousand years hence, who would know what the Medici had looked like. Thus he implied that his monuments would long outlast all memory of the subjects. Indeed, contemplation was more a characteristic of Giuliano. The sarcophagi

---

1524 (January). Models for tombs of Lorenzo and Giuliano begun.

1524 (spring). Models for statues.

1525. *Thought* (Lorenzo) begun.

1525–6. *Night, Dawn,* and two other figures (*Day, Twilight?*) almost completed. Models for four others (abandoned river gods) done.

1526. Tomb of Lorenzo built. Tomb of Giuliano started about June 30.

1528–30. Michelangelo occupied with defenses of Florence and siege of Florence.

1531 (summer). Two statues finished; third begun.

1531–4. *Thought* finished.

1532. Models for *St. Cosmas* and *St. Damian.*

1533 (July). *Action* (Giuliano) given to Montorsorli for finishing. Completed 1533–4.

1534 (September). Michelangelo ends all work on chapel. Montelupo completes *St. Damian.*

1536–7. Montorsorli completes *St. Cosmas.*

Tomb of Lorenzo de' Medici—*Thought* (Medici Chapel, San Lorenzo,
Florence)

were opened in 1875, however, at which time it was proved that Lorenzo does lie beneath the helmeted statue.

Instead, the work is a profound interpretation in three-dimensional marble of the power and meaning of thought. The individual spectator can probe its meaning only to the degree in which his emotions are aroused by the effect the figure has upon his senses. For the personality of the sculptor—the tormented human being named Michelangelo—is nowhere apparent in this awesome personalization of thought itself. The beauty and the grandeur of the statue lies in its being a self-portrait of thought, which existed before time, and will outlast it.

The brooding figure towers above the gigantic marbles of *Twilight* (the nude male on the spectator's left) and of *Dawn* (the female nude on his right) that recline on the lid of the sarcophagus below it. These allegories of physical time seem possessed of great sadness and despair, as if they sensed the futility of marking off brief periods of eternity. Their heroic proportions are ironic, for they themselves are merely conveniences. It is only man's thought that gives them dignity and purpose. As in the Sistine Chapel ceiling, there is a sense of the pervading intelligence of the universe, to which "a thousand years are but as yesterday when it is past" (Psalm 90:4).

Facing the genius of contemplation is the statue personifying action, the corollary of thought. This sits above the sarcophagus containing the mortal remains of Duke Giuliano. Here, the powerful, bareheaded male figure, dressed also in formfitting armor, seems about to leap to his feet. The springy grace of the elegant figure, which contrasts with its ponderous counterpart, expresses thought made concrete in action. One hand grasps a general's baton (which would more properly belong to the soldierly Lorenzo than to the easygoing Giuliano). The other hand holds a few coins as if about to toss them away—the squandering of thought in deeds. Here is the essence of force.

Tomb of Giuliano de' Medici—*Action* (Medici Chapel, San Lorenzo, Florence)

Michelangelo's subtle imagination presents it seated and static, hence terrifying in its suggestion of what it might be if released.

Beneath it recline two other gigantic nudes: *Day,* the male on the spectator's right; *Night,* the female on his left. These too are symbols of the factor of time in human life. *Day* is rolling over in a furious contortion, ready to burst into action. *Night* seems to be stirring uneasily in her sleep, as if troubled by unconscious recollections of action. The mask on which she leans suggests the disguise that night puts on actions; her poppies, the drugged mind that sees actions as other than they are; the owl, the alert mind that sees through concealment. (These symbols indicate that *Night* may have been the first of the six tomb statues to be executed; in the others, Michelangelo relied on character alone to express his concepts.)

Both of the seated figures face the tender *Madonna,* as if to suggest that she looks with pity and understanding on the strivings of man in thought and action. Michelangelo spent ten years trying to bring this noble concept to completion; the face is not quite finished. In that face is longing, as if the Virgin were looking toward the joy that will come when time and struggles will be no more. Her infant snuggles against her breast, his face buried as in the *Madonna of the Stairs.* But this *Madonna* is not, as it were, in a world of her own. She is deeply and compassionately concerned; her crossed legs, and the animated pose of the Child, suggest their vital involvement with the grief and frustration of human efforts.

It is doubtful that Michelangelo ever saw the elements of the Medici Chapel, perhaps the most eloquent expression of his deep emotions, assembled as he envisioned the ensemble—a testimony to his understanding of the trinity of life, death, and time. The marbles were not placed in position until 1545, when the bodies of the Medici were reinterred in the sarcophagi, and the chapel opened to the public. But it was not finished in

Madonna of the Medici Chapel (Medici Chapel, San Lorenzo, Florence)

Michelangelo's lifetime. There were to have been frescoes on the walls, and more statues in the niches. In 1556 the bright painting by Giovanni da' Udine on the interior of the dome was whitewashed over. The absence of decoration and the gray and white stone make the chapel colder in feeling than Michelangelo had intended it to be.

On September 23, 1534, Michelangelo arrived in Rome at the command of Pope Clement VII. The pope wanted Michelangelo near him in person for, as Condivi says, Clement "respected this man like one sacred and talked with him familiarly, on subjects both grave and gay, as he would have done with his equals."

Before he left Florence, Michelangelo wrote a friend that he would never return—perhaps a premonition. For on September 25, Pope Clement VII died. Without his protection, Michelangelo did not dare risk the hostility of Duke Alessandro de' Medici.

IX: DAYS OF RECKONING

Pope Clement VII was scarcely buried beside his cousin Pope
Leo X, in the Church of Santa Maria sopra Minerva, when the
Sacred College chose Alessandro Farnese to succeed him. On
October 13, 1534, the new pope took the name of Paul III, and
began his pontificate of fifteen years.

The sixty-six-year-old pope had been made a cardinal thirty
years earlier, in the reign of the Borgia Pope Alexander VI,
from whom he had learned many of his customs and proce-
dures. He was a learned man and a clever one, a shrewd
diplomat who was very careful about committing himself to a
yes or a no, a foresighted man, and as much a dedicated patron
of the arts as his predecessors. He quickly invited Michelangelo
to work for him.

The death of Clement VII, which brought to an end Michelangelo's work on the Medici projects in Florence, had led the
artist to hope that at last he could work uninterruptedly at his
cherished, if burdensome, assignment, the everlasting tomb of
Julius II. He pleaded with Pope Paul to be allowed to fulfill this
long-standing obligation.

"I am not my own master, Your Holiness," he said.

The new pope showed that he could fly into a rage as quickly
as Julius II. "It is thirty years that I have cherished this desire,"

he shouted, "and now that I am pope, may I not indulge it? Where is the contract? I mean to tear it up."

By this time Michelangelo was too used to the stormy temper of popes to be terrified into submission. He knew from experience that he could terrify them. At the age of nearly sixty years, he felt that he was already old—he had been complaining of that for many years—and might be nearing the end of his days. Besides he knew that Pope Paul was determined to carry out Pope Clement's idea of having Michelangelo fresco the west wall of the Sistine Chapel. Thus Michelangelo would have to abandon sculpture for painting again, and he was as unwilling to make this shift now as he had been with Pope Julius II.

Consequently, Michelangelo protested vigorously that he was under obligation to the heirs of Pope Julius. When the pope would not listen to this argument, Michelangelo resolved to move to Genoa, which was near the Carrara quarries, at last open to him again, or to Urbino, a pleasant and secluded mountain town, where the Della Roveres, the rulers of the district, would surely encourage his work on their monument.

Learning of this intention on the part of the artist he wanted, Pope Paul responded with the strategy for which he was famous. With eight of his cardinals he paid a visit to Michelangelo's house in the Macello de' Corvi. The whole entourage went out of their way to admire the work they saw there. And when Cardinal Ercole Gonzaga of Mantua saw the *Moses,* he exclaimed: "That piece alone is enough to do honor to the monument of Julius."

Pope Paul agreed. He renewed his requests, but Michelangelo would not budge. Michelangelo then changed his tone, "hoping," as Condivi says, "to pacify His Holiness with fair words." The pope would not budge. Finally the pope declared that he would see to it that the Della Roveres would be satisfied with three statues by Michelangelo, and would take the rest

from other hands. He promised to have a new contract negotiated with the heirs of Pope Julius. Then Michelangelo capitu-
lated.

It was seven years, however, before that new contract was
drawn up on August 30, 1542, and signed in the late fall of that
year. Meanwhile the young representative of the Della Rovere
interests found it expedient to relax the family pressure on
Michelangelo and to oblige Pope Paul by not interfering with
his assignments to the artist.

On September 1, 1535, Pope Paul III formally appointed
Michelangelo a member of his household, with a place at his
table, and a generous annual salary. The document also appointed him chief architect, sculptor, and painter to the Vatican. He thus was no more his own master than before.

At this time of his life, Michelangelo was lean and broad-
shouldered, with a wide forehead, a flat nose due to Torrigiano's
fist, yellow-brown eyes, thick black hair, and a forked beard. He
was of medium height. He lived simply, but not in the slovenly
fashion his own humorous remarks have led some biographers
to believe. He considered his house in Rome suitable for receiving an ambassador, but he remained fond of country food and
simple wines. He knew good cloth and insisted upon it for his
clothes, which he had carefully tailored. He habitually wore
fine linen shirts, a black damask doublet, a velvet cap of an old-
fashioned design, and cordovan boots which he had made to his
own specifications.

The decoration of the end walls of the Sistine Chapel had
been broached to Michelangelo by Pope Clement VII, probably
when they met on September 22, 1533. At that time Clement
seems to have had in mind a *Resurrection of Christ* for the west
(altar) wall, and a *Fall of the Rebel Angels* for the east
(entrance) wall. By December 10, 1533, Michelangelo had
been definitely commissioned for these works, and by February

20, 1534, he had begun sketches. By that time, however, the original idea for a *Resurrection of Christ* had apparently been reinterpreted, either by Pope Clement or Michelangelo, as a universal resurrection or *Last Judgment*. The latter subject undoubtedly appealed to a pope like Clement whose authority had been seriously challenged, for it would serve as a reminder to the unfaithful of the punishment awaiting them on the final day of the world. The same thought probably inspired Clement to wish a *Fall of the Rebel Angels* as well.

After the death of Clement and the almost immediate election of Pope Paul III, Michelangelo seems to have pretended to the new pope that he was working on cartoons for the second set of Sistine Chapel frescoes, although he was, in all probability, actually working on the sculptures for the tomb of Julius II. At any rate, when Pope Paul visited Michelangelo's house, probably in the spring of 1535, he saw the artist's sketches. The pope, says Condivi, "having meditated much on these things, finally resolved to have Michelangelo do the Last Judgment." It was to be executed on the west wall of the chapel.

That altar wall already had two windows, and also two frescoes by Perugino, as well as an altar piece and, above the windows, two lunettes by Michelangelo himself of the ancestors of Christ.

Dismissing from his mind any thought of compromise, Michelangelo proceeded to have all these works scraped off, the windows blocked up, and the wall resurfaced so that it would slant inward from the ceiling and thus help prevent his fresco from gathering dust. This labor was carried out by Michelangelo's beloved assistant, Francesco d'Amadore, known as Urbino, whom he had engaged in 1533 and who stayed with him the rest of his life.

It was not until May of 1536, therefore, that Michelangelo once more climbed up on a scaffolding in the Sistine Chapel.

He began the huge fresco, which was 66 × 33 feet at the top, with the group of angels who carry the symbols of Christ's Passion. By February 4, 1537, the work was far enough along for Pope Paul to inspect it. After that visit, word got around as to the nature of Michelangelo's undertaking. On September 15, 1537, the dreaded critic of the age, Pietro Aretino, presumed to write Michelangelo his theories of what a fresco of the Last Judgment should be.

Aretino, having failed as a painter, had become an art dealer. Thus he knew artists well, especially the great Venetian master Titian. He was also a poet and a prose writer of genius—and of a wit so ferocious that crowned heads feared him. In fact, he was known as the "scourge of princes." Above all, he was a cynic, and at the end of his flamboyant life it could be said of him:

> He had aped every moral attitude. Honor and glory and religion and virtue and patriotism and pride—he had imitated them all and the world had accepted and applauded his counterfeit. He had struck every pose and discarded it and paraded its opposite, and the world had accepted and applauded his performance. He had impersonated every virtue and made it unmeaning. (Roeder, *The Man of the Renaissance*.)

During the Renaissance period it was not unusual for a learned man, perhaps a poet, or a theologian, to advise a painter on his subject matter, for artists were seldom educated men. Many years before, Michelangelo may have taken Poliziano's advice for his *Battle of the Centaurs*, but since then he had expanded his knowledge, his spirit, and his imagination. His concepts came from sounder foundations than Aretino's rather decadent ones. He replied to Aretino's letter with typical irony:

Magnificent Messer Pietro, my lord and brother—The
receipt of your letter has caused me at once both pleasure
and regret. I was exceedingly pleased because it came from
you, who are uniquely gifted among men, and yet I was
also very regretful because, having completed a large part of
the composition, I cannot put your conception in hand,
which is so perfect that, if the Day of Judgment were
passed and you had seen it in person, your words could not
have described it better.

Now as to your writing about me, I not only say in reply
that I should welcome it, but I entreat you to do so, since
kings and emperors deem it the highest honor to be mentioned by your pen. In the meantime, should I have
anything that might be to your taste, I offer it to you with
all my heart.

In conclusion, do not, for the sake of seeing the painting I am doing, break your resolve not to come to Rome,
because that would be too much. I commend me to you.

Aretino really wanted a drawing by Michelangelo, either to
sell or to add to his collection of works of art. Michelangelo
refused to send anything by his hand to this rapacious Venetian
connoisseur. Disappointed, Aretino began to disparage Michelangelo and, in November, 1545, after *The Last Judgment* was
finished, sent him a scurrilous letter which attacked not only
the fresco itself but Michelangelo's honesty, his private life, and
his attitudes. It had considerable effect on Michelangelo's
spirits.

For in spite of his tendency to quarrel, Michelangelo was a
courteous man, and expected courtesy from others. The intrigue
he found about him made him suspicious, especially now that
he had grown old, but he showed to others the same kindness,
generosity, and consideration that he craved for himself. Al-

though he might be disgusted with a person, he would instruct his family to spare that person's feelings as they straightened out the matter for him. His patience, especially with stupidity, was, however, soon exhausted. He was a perfectionist, something that those who worked for him seldom appreciated. He himself said that his workmen found him "in some way strange and obsessed." Many of them hated him and vilified him, but he was very kind to those who were big enough to love him and be loyal to him.

"Strange and obsessed" Michelangelo was indeed, and as a result he was lonely. He craved friends, and almost worshiped those in whom, like Tommaso Cavalieri, he saw beauty of person and character. To his friend Luigi del Riccio, he said in declining an invitation to dinner: "I am a man more inclined than anyone who ever lived to care for people. Whenever I see anyone possessed of some gift which shows him to be more apt in the performance or expression of anything than others, I become, perforce, enamored of him and am constrained to abandon myself to him in such a way that I am no longer my own, but wholly his."

He added that if he gave himself to his friends at the dinner party, he would be "torn away from himself and therefore confused for days." In other words, he needed to get away from his associates for a while in order to return to himself.

Michelangelo's friends during this rich and artistically satisfying period of his life in Rome were chiefly former Florentines like himself. They were, in a way, self-exiles. They detested the tyranny of the later Medici over their native city; they deplored the loss of Florentine liberty to those tyrants; and, like Michelangelo, they feared the reprisals of the vicious Alessandro de' Medici if they should return to the Florence he ruled so despotically.

But on the night of January 5, 1537, Alessandro was murdered by his twenty-two-year-old cousin and companion in profligacy, Lorenzino de' Medici. After this act, Lorenzino fled to Venice. The Florentine exiles there hailed him as the liberator of their city. Soon, wherever the Florentine expatriates had gathered, the half-insane Lorenzino was regarded as a savior of liberty no less distinguished than the Brutus who had stabbed the ambitious dictator Julius Caesar in 44 B.C. The analogy was far from accurate, but exiled patriots are generally too emotional to respect the facts of history.

Donato Gianotti, a Florentine political writer and literary man, was one of Michelangelo's circle of friends in Rome. Gianotti proposed that, in commemoration of Lorenzino's "liberation" of Florence, Michelangelo carve a bust of Brutus, which Gianotti would present to his patron, Cardinal Niccolò Ridolfi.

This thirty-inch-high marble bust, now in the Bargello in Florence, is a grand and noble conception of a man whose egotism has led him to violate the sanctity of the established order. For the institution of government Michelangelo had an almost religious reverence, something he may have got from Dante. The human embodiment of sovereignty was another matter. The *Brutus* shows this conflict of conscience—on the one hand, selfless heroism; on the other hand, ruthless arrogance. The roughly finished face is full of tension between sensitivity and brutality. In contrast is the highly polished toga into which the bull neck disappears. No portrait of any individual, the *Brutus* is a profoundly understood portrait of a type of human nature, and is perhaps the best example of Michelangelo's gift of psychological penetration.

Of all his friends in Rome the most influential was the remarkable woman he met probably in 1536. This was the Marchesa Vittoria Colonna, fifteen years younger than he. For eleven years this member of the powerful Colonna family had

Brutus (Bargello, Florence)

Michelangelo's drawing of Vittoria Colonna

been the widow of the brilliant but unscrupulous Marchese di Pescara, whom she had dearly loved. Grief over the death of this military man in 1525, and disillusionment over the sack of Rome in 1527, had induced her to choose a life of retirement. Most of the time she lived as a secular nun in the convent of San Silvestro in Rome (Number 9 of the present Via XXIV Maggio, near the Piazza Quirinale). There Michelangelo frequently visited her—it was not far from his house—and there, perhaps on the charming roof garden of the convent, took place, in October, 1538, the three famous conversations which the Portuguese miniaturist Francisco d'Ollanda recorded in his *Dialogues*—probably the most reliable data on Michelangelo's opinions about art.

Vittoria Colonna was a capable poet who expressed herself with simplicity and sincerity. She loved and understood works of art. She was also deeply interested in religion, and corresponded with the leading theologians of her time. At first inclined to question strict orthodoxy to the point of risking trial for heresy by the Inquisition, she later supported the great revival of Catholicism, known as the Counter-Reformation, which Pope Paul III did much to inspire. She was one of the few persons, and certainly the only woman, whom Michelangelo considered anything near an intellectual equal.

Michelangelo still retained much of the spirit of humanism that he had absorbed in the household of Lorenzo the Magnificent. Platonism was a strong influence on his work in the Medici Chapel. The new emotional spirit of the Counter-Reformation challenged that calmer philosophy. The conflict perplexed the profoundly religious Michelangelo. He turned to Vittoria Colonna for guidance. In one of the several poems he addressed to her, Michelangelo says:

First on my right foot, then upon my left,
I shift my searches for salvation.
My heart grows tired as I waver between vices and virtues,

And I am like one who, with no glimpse of Heaven,
Misses every road in the darkness.
Here am I, a blank page, for you to pen your sacred writing
on . . .

Let me not live so blindly!
Tell me, sacred Lady,
Whether Heaven does honor sin repented
As well as unstained good.

Michelangelo became spiritually dependent on this noble-hearted woman, who knew how to handle him. He responded to the beauty of her character—for she seems not to have been physically beautiful—with the same love he felt for every expression of divine perfection. He had at last found a spirit to commune with.

Their mutual devotion, being of this pure nature, did not disturb Michelangelo's need to belong to himself and his work, for it made no demands upon him. Instead, Michelangelo found the marchesa a stabilizing force. She, too, had felt the uncertainty of a truly concerned person as to man's spiritual survival in a world that had become unstable.

The expansion of the world they had known as children through the discovery of the Western Hemisphere; Martin Luther's challenging of old religious beliefs; the catastrophe of the sack of Rome; Copernicus' scientific reversal of man's notions of the solar system, probably known to intellectuals as early as 1530—all these had destroyed the solidity of mature thinking people's faith in an established, supposedly unchangeable order of things.

Out of doubts as to the certainty of God's care for the world, Vittoria Colonna developed a pure and simple faith in man's salvation. This she imparted to Michelangelo. He began to see that salvation is a present as well as a future state. He acknowledged her spiritual gift in the works he made for her—a Crucifixion, a *Pietà*, and a Christ with the Woman of Samaria.

These paintings, which have disappeared, though copies of them exist, had in common the theme of spiritual regeneration through faith in Christ's love and sacrifice. Particularly revealing of Michelangelo's spiritual adjustment is his choice of Christ and the Woman of Samaria as a subject, for in the Gospel account of that interview are Christ's words: "Whosoever drinketh of the water that I shall give him shall never thirst; but the water that I shall give him shall be in him a well of water springing up into everlasting life" (John 4:14). This "water" refreshed and reinvigorated Michelangelo's troubled spirit in those days of reckoning that the changing times demanded.

In acknowledging that gift, the marchesa wrote to Michelangelo on July 20, 1542, that she was "praying that Lord of Whom you spoke to me with such a fervent and humble heart, on my departure from Rome, that I may find you on my return with His image so renewed and alive by true faith in your soul, as you have so well painted it in my Woman of Samaria."

That spiritual adjustment was in process at the same time that Michelangelo was executing the fresco of *The Last Judgment*. Although he had made designs for the fresco before he met the Marchesa di Pescara, and the fresco is basically close to these, his new attitude toward religion had much to do with the actual manner in which he expressed in it his thoughts and feelings about man's fate.

The fresco was unveiled on the eve of All Saints' Day, October 31, 1541, when Pope Paul III celebrated vespers in the

Sistine Chapel, exactly twenty-nine years after Michelangelo's ceiling had been unveiled there. Then all the debris of the scaffolding was removed from the chapel, and *The Last Judgment* was shown to the public on Christmas Day. A huge throng crowded into the chapel for that official inauguration.

What that crowd beheld was a mighty swarm of human bodies whirled as by a tempest around a central void of stormy blue. Probably their first reaction was one of holy fear, and they felt the terrible reality of the *Dies Irae* ("Day of Wrath"), the thirteenth-century hymn whose somber verses boomed at every mass for the dead. Vasari, who had made the long journey from Venice to inspect his master's latest work, says: "I along with the rest was stupefied by what I saw."

His initial stupefaction over, the scrutinizing spectator should first perceive a group of angels with trumpets (Revelation 8:11). They hover in the lower central section of the fresco, just above the gulf that divides the green earth at the left from the murky Hell at the right. Here is, as it were, the label of the painting, proclaimed by the "seventh angel" of the vision of St. John: ". . . thy wrath is come, and the time of the dead, that they should be judged, and that thou shouldest give reward unto thy servants the prophets, and to the saints, and them that fear thy name, small and great, and shouldest destroy them which destroy the earth" (Revelation 11:18).

The spectator's eye should then move to the left arc of the ellipse of the composition. For the motion of the painting is a kind of planetary orbit about the central sunlike figure of Christ the judge. On the left the dead rise from their graves. Helped by angels and the spirits of those already reborn, they ascend into a cloud-based sphere. There prophets and saints mill around a sunburst in which is silhouetted the Son of Man, who has, as he foretold, "come in the glory of his Father with his

The Last Judgment (Sistine Chapel, Rome)

angels; and then he shall reward every man according to his works" (Matthew 16:27).

Above this sphere, in the former lunettes, are those angels of Christ's own prophecy. They carry the symbols of His Passion, His sacrifice for the forgiveness of man's sins.

In the throng of patriarchs and prophets, sibyls and saints, Michelangelo has singled out a few for identification by the symbols of their life or martyrdom. On the left are the favorite saints of Florence: Mary Magdalene (welcoming a saved soul); John the Baptist (lambskins); Andrew (X-shaped cross); and, below, Lawrence (grill). On the right are the favorite saints of Rome and of the Church in general. St. Peter (keys) leads these. At his right foot are St. Simon the Zealot (saw); St. Philip (cross); St. Blaise (combs of nails); St. Catherine of Alexandria (spiked wheel); St. Sebastian (arrows); St. Simon of Cyrene (carrying cross). Below these, balancing St. Lawrence, is St. Bartholomew (knife).

From St. Bartholomew's left hand dangles his own skin. (His martyrdom involved his being flayed alive.) On this skin Michelangelo painted a caricature of himself to indicate his own "flaying" by hostile critics. St. Bartholomew looks very much like Pietro Aretino.

The Virgin crouches at the right of Christ. She looks only at the saved, who have implored her intercession. Her humble pose implies that she can do nothing for those who have ignored her. Being the symbol of purity, she cannot see their impurity.

On the spectator's right, the bodies of the damned hurtle, or are dragged by demons, down to eternal suffering in Hell. Their faces and their postures show less terror of their fate than sorrow over the recognition that they have misused their lives. They have destroyed the earth rather than improved it.

Below them is Hell, as Dante experienced it in his *Inferno*. Here the wicked are beaten by the oar of a fiendish Charon,

who ferries them toward a serpent-entwined Minos for assignment to an everlasting torture ironically similar to the torment
in which they spent their earthly lives.

Minos, at the extreme lower right, is a portrait of Pope Paul
III's master of ceremonies, Biagio da Cesena. This officious
courtier thought the nudity of the fresco, which he inspected
with the pope before it was finished, shameful. He declared the
work "fit not for a papal church but rather for the public baths
and taverns."

Michelangelo's revenge for this gratuitous criticism was to
immortalize Cesena—in Hell, and with asses' ears.

The chamberlain protested to the pope, beseeching him to
make Michelangelo remove the likeness. When Michelangelo
refused, Pope Paul said pithily:

"Had he put you in Purgatory, I might have helped you, but
I have no authority in Hell."

Such little revenges are minor examples of Michelangelo's
intensely personal feeling about this climactic moment in the
tragic drama of man's existence. Like Dante, he accepted as a
parable the traditional projection of the scrupulous man's
dreaded time of reckoning with himself. This projection is the
"Day of Wrath," the prophecy of Ezekiel (Ezekiel 27:5–10)
and the fearful vision of the author of Revelation: "voices, and
thunderings, and lightnings, and an earthquake . . . hail and
fire mingled with blood." For the time in one's life of balancing
one's spiritual accounts is as inevitable as taxes and as much to
be dreaded.

Also like Dante, Michelangelo conceived the future punish-
ments or rewards of man in no different terms from the torment—or the process of atonement and reform, or the bliss—
which a man experiences in his earthly life "according to his
works." He retained all the stage scenery of the allegory, but he
invested it with his own thinking about man's fate. Here he

reached at last the harmony of pagan humanism and Christian faith he had so long sought.

The key to Michelangelo's thinking is his concept of Christ the judge. His Christ has the heroic figure and pose of the pagan Phoebus Apollo, the spirit of creative imagination. Yet His virile, athletic body bears the marks of His human suffering for the redemption of sinful man. He has triumphed over these and become the true God-man. His powerful, upraised right hand draws the virtuous to Him with an energy of its own. They rise, not with wings, but of their own power. The gentler gesture of Christ's left hand brushes the sinful away rather than dooms them to perdition. His expression is not one of wrath but of understanding—the recognition that no man is wholly virtuous or wholly wicked.

Michelangelo thus implies that the creative imagination, the human reflection of God's creative power, is the redeeming force. It summons man's virtues to aid him in realizing himself; it dismisses the impeding faults. The individual man is, therefore, his own judge. It is up to him and him alone to have faith in his own redeeming goodness, which is his share of God's goodness. This faith is necessary, for the share is small and the faults are many—witness the small book of the saved and the enormous book of the damned which the trumpeting angels of *The Last Judgment* carry.

At the unveiling Pope Paul is said to have fallen on his knees in penitential prayer before this supreme expression of God's creative power extended in man. *The Last Judgment* has caused many another spectator to repent his shortcomings and pray that he may surmount them. Only those who have lost all faith in themselves, all hope of eventually completing themselves, in short all striving for happiness, can stand before it and not feel a sacred, purifying, elevating terror of the judgment they must ultimately pass upon themselves.

The bottom space of *The Last Judgment* below the sphere of earth and Hell, was cut away to provide for a reredos (ornamental screen) and two doors. The colors, none too bright at any time, have dimmed, except at the still radiant top where Christ shines in glory beneath the space-defying angels of the Passion. The prudery of a later age demanded that the nudity of some figures be covered with tasteless drapery. Still the vast fresco seems everlastingly contemporary and, along with the ceiling above it, the nearest art can come to solving the mystery of the identity of man and God.

X: FROM CARVING
TO BUILDING

Creating *The Last Judgment* drained even Michelangelo's superhuman intellectual and physical energies. During the spring of 1541 he had fallen from the scaffolding in the Sistine Chapel and had hurt his leg. "In his pain and anger," wrote Vasari, "he refused to be treated by anyone. But a doctor, Baccio Rontini, forced his way into Michelangelo's house and would not leave the injured artist until he had cured him." Nevertheless, by August, 1541, before *The Last Judgment* was finished, Paul III was hounding Michelangelo to paint two frescoes on the walls of the chapel the pope was having built in the Vatican by Antonio da Sangallo the Younger.

Before the chapel was ready for frescoing, Michelangelo had some time to devote to the tomb of Julius II. It had been agreed that Michelangelo himself was to finish only the *Moses* and two other statues; the rest, and the architecture of the monument, were to be done by other hands. By July, 1542, Michelangelo was already well along on these two statues—*Leah* and *Rachel*. But by then the chapel was ready. Consequently Michelangelo petitioned the pope to intercede with the Della Roveres that the two statues be finished by Raffaello da Montelupo.

Months went by before the fourth contract was ratified by the dukes of Urbino. There was great question over which party owed money to the other. This frustration, plus the pope's nagging, drove Michelangelo to burst out in exasperation, in a letter to Cardinal Alessandro Farnese, the pope's grandson: "I am stoned every day, as if I had crucified Christ. . . . I lost the whole of my youth, chained to this Tomb, contending, as far as I was able, against the demands of Popes Leo and Clement. . . . I am not a thieving usurer."

Finally the Della Roveres refused Michelangelo's request. Somehow, however, he found time to complete these statues, probably before the end of 1542.

The two heavily robed figures of women show a loss of energy in Michelangelo's invention. The forms of the bodies are plain beneath the drapery, but they have little of the dramatic vitality that characterizes Michelangelo's previous sculpture. They are, in fact, rather lifeless, as if the artist were scarcely involved emotionally or intellectually with his subject. The endless arguments, delays, and alterations in the design of the tomb had obviously sapped his enthusiasm for the monument.

In medieval theology Leah and Rachel, the two wives of the patriarch Jacob and hence the mothers of the tribes of Israel, represent respectively the active and the contemplative life. This allegory Michelangelo somewhat followed in his representation of the two sisters, but it is a blunted conception compared to the *Thought* and *Action* of the Medici Chapel. Possibly the real reason for the decline in Michelangelo's imagination from those two commanding figures in Florence is the resolution in his own thinking of the conflict between his humanism and his Christianity. He no longer had a powerful inner tension to release. *Rachel* and *Leah* likewise have no inner force.

Michelangelo began the frescoes in the pope's new chapel (the Capella Paolina, or Pauline Chapel) in November, 1542.

The earlier, *The Conversion of St. Paul,* was finished in July, 1545. Owing to a fire in the chapel, which slightly damaged that fresco, Michelangelo did not begin the second, *The Crucifixion of St. Peter,* until March, 1546. During the years that Michelangelo labored "ill-content," as he himself said, on these paintings, the happiness he had known throughout the previous ten years began to fade.

On January 8, 1544, died the idol of the Florentine "exiles" in Rome, Francesco (Cecchino) de' Bracci, the first cousin once removed of Luigi del Riccio, Michelangelo's most intimate friend. The charming sixteen-year-old Francesco had seemed the hope of the patriots. At Riccio's request Michelangelo wrote forty-eight epitaphs to be circulated as a memorial to the youth, and designed his tomb for execution by Urbino. It is in the south transept of the Church of Santa Maria in Aracoeli.

In the early summer of 1544 Michelangelo fell so seriously ill of a fever that he made no protest when Luigi del Riccio took him from his own house to be cared for in the Riccio apartments in the palace of the Strozzi family, del Riccio's employers. Pope Paul sent daily to inquire after Michelangelo's health, and everyone of importance in Rome paid a visit. By the end of July, Michelangelo had recovered, but he was too old fully to regain all his former strength.

Six months later Michelangelo quarreled with del Riccio over that devoted friend and business agent's having authorized a cheap engraving of a portrait of the artist. The dispute broke up their plans to make a pilgrimage to the shrine of St. James in Compostela, Spain, in the spring of 1545. Doubtless this would have been Michelangelo's gesture of thanks for his recovery. But they patched up their differences and remained friends.

In February, 1545, the tomb of Julius II was finally erected, complete with statues, in the Church of San Pietro in Vincoli. Michelangelo must have looked with aching sadness at this

travesty of his dreams of forty years before. For the statues
executed by the facile Montelupo are uninspired, and the whole
monument, except for the *Moses,* is rather insipid.

At the end of the year, Michelangelo was ill again. Again
Luigi del Riccio nursed him back to health in the Strozzi
palace. Out of gratitude to this friend, who had twice saved his
life, Michelangelo gave him *The Rebellious Slave* and *The
Dying Slave,* which had never found their proper place on the
tomb of Julius II.

Luigi del Riccio died in the autumn of 1546. Thereafter,
Michelangelo, thinking it unbearable to have the statues back,
sent them to France, as a gift to Roberto Strozzi, who had been
his absent host. Later Strozzi tactfully gave them to King
Francis I of France.

For that monarch had written to Michelangelo, asking for
something by his hand and also for casts of the *Christ* in Santa
Maria sopra Minerva and the *Pietà* in St. Peter's. On April 26,
1546, Michelangelo replied in a touching letter:

Sacred Majesty—I know not which is the greater, the
favor or the wonder that Your Majesty should deign to
write to a man like me, and still further to request of him
examples of his work, which are in no way worthy of Your
Majesty's name. But such as they are, be it known to Your
Majesty that for a long time I have desired to serve you,
but have been unable to do so, because even in Italy I have
not had sufficient opportunities to devote myself to my
art.

Now I am an old man and shall be engaged for some
months on work for the Pope. But if, on its completion, a
little of life remains to me, I will endeavor to put into
effect the desire which, as I have said, I have had for a long
time, that is to say to execute for Your Majesty a work in

marble, in bronze, and in painting. But if death balks me
in this desire of mine, I will not fail to fulfill it in the next
life, where no one longer grows old, if it be possible to
carve and to paint there. And I pray God to give Your
Majesty a long and happy life.

The letter may reflect a loyalty Michelangelo felt to the pope
and to his country. Perhaps this had been rekindled by the
great honor which he received on March 20, 1546. Then, in an
impressive ceremony on the Capitoline Hill, he was declared a
citizen of Rome. Perhaps he felt that he should not work for a
foreign ruler who had not always been on peaceful terms with
the papacy.

By the time of that ceremony, the transformation of the
desolate plateau between the two peaks of the Capitoline Hill
into a city center had been in progress for about nine years.

The city fathers of the twelfth century had dreamed of restoring the former glory of their city when they chose the Capitoline, the citadel of ancient Rome, as the site of the civic
government. There, on the remains of the Tabularium (Ar-
chives Building) erected in 78 B.C., they built the castle which
is now, much remodeled, the Palazzo Senatorio, the office of the
governor of Rome. It is on the east side of the plateau.

To the left (south) of that municipal center had been built,
about 1450, a palace for the offices of what would today be the
city commissioners—the Palazzo dei Conservatori. This pair of
structures was accessible only from the earliest Roman Forum,
to the east. The later city, however, had grown up on the banks
of the Tiber, to the west. There was, therefore, little connection
between this isolated seat of the city government and the city
itself.

When the Emperor Charles V was about to make a triumphal entry into Rome in 1536, the pope razed the slums that

surrounded the Capitoline in order to provide a suitable avenue for welcoming the emperor. This renovation seems to have given a group of public-spirited citizens the idea for making a new communal center on the very spot which once had been the center of Rome. They easily persuaded Pope Paul III to effect it. In the following year the Pope, as a beginning, had the ancient bronze equestrian statue of the Emperor Marcus Aurelius (A.D. 121–180) moved from the Piazza di Laterano to the plateau.

Even though Michelangelo had opposed the shift, Pope Paul directed him to design a pedestal for this superb statue, which was set up on the Capitoline in 1538. Actually, Michelangelo only altered for the better the existing base. While engaged on this assignment he probably conceived the plan of the magnificent complex now known as the Campidoglio. For Pope Paul had undoubtedly asked him to make proposals for a city center on the Capitoline which would include an access from the city, a level paved area for ceremonies, and restoration of the shabby old structures already on the plateau.

The project was not completed for over one hundred years, but only a few changes were made in Michelangelo's original plans. These called for the noble ramp of shallow steps on the western slope of the hill, by which the visitor now approaches the plaza. At the top is a balustrade that defines the open end of the area. On this are eighteen-foot-high Roman statues of Castor and Pollux, the twin patron divinities of ancient Rome, and also trophies, ancient statues of Constantine and Constans, and columns.

The area itself Michelangelo designed as a trapezoid. Its northern and southern sides slope inward toward the Palazzo Senatorio, the focal point of the complex. The eye of the visitor ascending the ramp is, therefore, directed to that building both by the statue of Marcus Aurelius, located in an oval depression

The Campidoglio, Rome

in the center of the area, and by the oval pattern of the pavement. Michelangelo derived that design from contemporary charts of the orbits of the celestial bodies.

The buildings that line the sloping sides are twins: the Palazzo dei Conservatori on the visitor's right (south) and, facing it, the Palazzo Nuovo, now the Capitoline Museum. The design of the pavement also brings these buildings into organic unity with the ramp, the statue, and the Palazzo Senatorio.

For the facade of that central building Michelangelo designed a double staircase which rises in a broken outline to a loggia in the middle of the building. This is above a niche that contains an ancient statue of Minerva (rechristened Roma). In the triangles formed by the two flights of stairs Michelangelo placed ancient statues of river gods—the Tiber or Tigris (right) and the Nile (left).

Michelangelo remodeled the Palazzo dei Conservatori, giving it an open portico of wide bays that frame the actual building. The columns of these bays continue the vertical line begun by the columns (ancient mileposts from the Appian Way) on the balustrade. The figures on the cornice continue the sculptural feeling of the entire plaza from the colossal statues that frame the top of the ramp. The Palazzo Nuovo, naturally, duplicated this effect.

The result is a breathtaking setting for the solemn and stately public rituals for which the whole project was intended. After Michelangelo's death, Tommaso dei Cavalieri carried on the master's plans for it.

Antonio da Sangallo the Younger died on August 3, 1546. At that time he was engaged in building, according to his own designs, the Rome residence of Pope Paul III's family, the Farnese Palace, now the French Embassy, on the Piazza Farnese. He had also been the chief architect of St. Peter's, the structure of which he had considerably altered from the first design of Bramante, and the later ones of Raphael and Baldassare Peruzzi.

Michelangelo had little admiration for Sangallo as an architect. He had already denounced Sangallo's design for the cornice of the Farnese Palace as "barbarous" and "dangerous to the structure." Consequently Pope Paul now announced a competition for new designs for the cornice. Michelangelo's submission pleased the pope the most, and in the autumn of 1546, he appointed Michelangelo to finish the structure.

A cornice is an important decorative part of a building in the classical style. It is the "frame" such a building requires in order to be aesthetically pleasing; it logically finishes off the top of the building to which the eye of the spectator has been directed by the lines of the structure itself. A cornice might, therefore, be compared to the capital of a tall column, or, perhaps, to the lid of an ornamental box.

As might be expected, Michelangelo had approached the problem from the point of view of a sculptor. He visualized the cornice as a load supported by a human figure—the building itself. The articulated—that is, interdependent—stresses are like those implicit in the *Atlas Slave*. The cornice he produced is sufficiently grand in its proportions to suggest the weight necessary to keep the walls upright; it gives the facade gravity and sobriety. Yet its lively ornament makes on this massive overhang a play of light and shade that gives it a feeling of weightlessness.

This same imaginative inventiveness Michelangelo carried over into the central window of the facade and also into the court of the Farnese Palace. In this private interior of the palace the ornamentation of the window frames and pediments is almost frivolous but still stately—dignity with a wink. The effect is a kind of satire on the conventional, dry, precise classi-

cal style. Lighter in spirit than Michelangelo's loosening-up of
that style in the Medici Chapel, this treatment of the court is
admirably suited to the sophistication of the Farnese family and
of the Roman atmosphere.

There was, naturally enough, violent opposition to Michelangelo on the part of the clique of Sangallo's previous associates.
These minor architects were afraid that the new techniques of
Sangallo's successor would deprive them of the subcommissions
that Sangallo had awarded them. Their very vocal hostility,
however, had no effect on Pope Paul III.

Michelangelo and Pope Paul were on easy and familiar terms
with each other. Michelangelo hated ceremony and the insin-
cerity that protocol demands. The pope found this attitude
refreshing, and he appreciated Michelangelo's simple gifts of
fruit and wine as much as the extravagant presents ambassadors
made him.

"Sometimes," Michelangelo told Francisco d'Ollanda, "my
important duties have given me so much license that when I am
talking to the Pope, I put this old felt hat nonchalantly on my
head and speak to him very frankly, but he does not put me to
death on that account."

By no means! In fact, the pope added to Michelangelo's
"important duties" by appointing him chief architect of St.
Peter's on January 1, 1547. Thus Michelangelo succeeded to
another position that Sangallo had held.

Michelangelo claimed that he was not an architect, just as he
had insisted to Pope Julius II that he was not a painter. The
pope practically had to command him to accept the appointment. His achievements in architectural design, however, only
emphasized his modesty.* And by this time he had had enough

* Earlier examples of Michelangelo's architectural designs that were
executed in structures which still exist are the facade of the Chapel of
Leo X in the Castel San Angelo, Rome (1514); the windows of the

experience in architecture to formulate a theory of design, which he expressed in a letter to a now unknown correspondent. In this letter he refers to his own plans for St. Peter's:

> When a plan has diverse parts, all those that are of the same character and dimension must be decorated in the same way and in the same manner; and their counterparts likewise. But when a plan changes its form entirely, it is not only permissible but necessary to vary the ornaments also and that of their counterparts likewise. The central features are always as independent as one chooses—just as the nose, being in the middle of the face, is related neither to one eye nor to the other, though one hand is certainly related to the other and one eye to the other, owing to their being at the sides and having counterparts.
>
> It is therefore indisputable that the limbs of architecture are derived from the limbs of man. No one who has not been or is not a good master of the human figure, particularly of anatomy, can comprehend this.

Michelangelo's purpose for St. Peter's was to seek the organic unity that he described in that letter. He proposed the elimination of Sangallo's abundance of details, and aimed at restoring the grandeur of Bramante's original conception. But before 1547 was out, the Sangallo clique was making trouble over Michelangelo's discarding of their master's intentions, which they could see might well destroy their own work as well as their commissions, and Michelangelo was harassed by their intrigues for the rest of his life.

Medici Palace, Florence (c. 1517); the Reliquary Tribune of San Lorenzo, Florence (1532); and, of course, the Medici Chapel (1520–34) and the Laurentian Library, Florence (1523–59).

In addition, Michelangelo was greatly saddened by the death, on February 25, 1547, of his spiritual guide, Vittoria Colonna. When he paid his last visit to her, he raised her lifeless hand to his lips. Afterward he regretted that he had not kissed her cheek and forehead too.

The multiplicity of Michelangelo's undertakings diverted him from his sorrow. He was superintending the new fortifications of the Vatican, a commission he had won from Pope Paul after bitter controversy with Sangallo. He was involved, in 1548, in another controversy—with the civic authorities of Rome over designs for repairing an ancient bridge across the Tiber in order to accommodate the expected throng of pilgrims in the Holy Year of 1550. The shortsighted commissioners took the project away from Michelangelo and gave it to the leader of the Sangallo clique, who promised them a more showy superstructure but did nothing about the shaky substructure. His bridge collapsed in a flood in 1555. Michelangelo was also occupied with his designs for St. Peter's and with those for the Campidoglio, and the execution of them. And he was still painting *The Crucifixion of St. Peter* in the Pauline Chapel of the Vatican.

On October 11, 1549, Pope Paul attempted to silence the Sangallo clique by conferring supreme powers on Michelangelo as the architect of St. Peter's. This decree meant, however, that now that Michelangelo had innumerable contracts and subcommissions to award, the Sangallo clique began accusing him of graft. Two years later he had to prove his honesty in having awarded these without bribes or kickbacks.

On October 13, 1549, the eighty-year-old pope visited the Pauline Chapel, and climbed up on the scaffolding to inspect *The Crucifixion of St. Peter*, which was by then almost finished. (Michelangelo completed it in 1550.) Presumably Pope Paul was pleased with this memorial of his tenure as St. Peter's

The Crucifixion of St. Peter (Pauline Chapel, Vatican City)

The Conversion of St. Paul (Pauline Chapel, Vatican City)

successor, and with its companion fresco, *The Conversion of St. Paul*, which commemorates his saintly namesake.

Later generations have been somewhat less than pleased with these twenty-foot-square frescoes. The *St. Paul* has some of the violent agitation of *The Last Judgment*, which it followed almost immediately, and it reflects the same concern of Michelangelo with faith. The *St. Paul*, however, lacks unity, being composed in two horizontal zones. Above, Christ with a company of angels plunges down from the sky like Jehovah separating the earth from the waters on the Sistine Chapel ceiling. Below, the smitten St. Paul lies on the ground, surrounded by his terror-stricken companions. The two contrasting levels are connected only vaguely—and rather awkwardly—by the bolting horse from which the saint has fallen. The message of the fresco is one of austere morality—the blindness of a man without faith. This gives the painting a storytelling quality that robs it of universality. It is little more than an illustration of Acts 8:1–9.

The composition of the *St. Peter* is simpler and calmer. But the facial expression and the twisted posture of the saint, whose martyrdom expresses the supreme proof of faith, make him seem wrathful at his fate. An old man, he has the awe-inspiring force of the *Moses*, but even Michelangelo could not render the unconventional pose anything but slightly ridiculous. (St. Peter asked to be crucified head downward, for he felt unworthy to suffer as his Master had done.) Hence, the bystanders' emotions of sorrow or reverent wonder are rather incongruous. Here again is an anecdote rather than a universal experience.

Nevertheless, there are many flashes of Michelangelo's old genius and his daring imagination in these last two paintings of his. Their total effect, however, is so disappointing that a close analysis of them seems futile. Furthermore, they are not available to the public; special permission must be obtained for a visit to the Pauline Chapel.

Less than a month after his visit to the Pauline Chapel, Pope Paul III died. "The death of the Pope," Michelangelo wrote, "has been a great sorrow to me and a loss no less, because I received many benefits from His Holiness and hoped to receive still more." He went on to say that Pope Paul "died a beautiful death and was conscious to the last."

The ability and the desire of a departing soul to make a last confession and to receive final absolution was a great concern of Michelangelo. He had mentioned this anxiety in connection with the deaths of members of his family, most recently that of his irresponsible brother Giovan Simone on January 9, 1548. A "state of perfect contrition," he believed, "suffices for salvation." He repeated these sentiments after the death of Gismondo Buonarroti on November 13, 1555. Old himself, Michelangelo dreaded the death of his soul—the "double death" he mentions in a sonnet. Some deep sense of guilt apparently troubled him. Perhaps this was what made him overscrupulous in his dealings with others.

Pope Paul III's successors, Julius III, Marcellus II, Paul IV, and Pius IV, confirmed Michelangelo's authority as chief architect of St. Peter's. This meant that he remained the dictator of all aesthetic matters in the control of the papacy; he had virtually the final word on art in the Christian world.

None of those popes, however, had the dedication to art that motivated Julius II, Leo X, Clement VII, and Paul III. Nor did they have the forceful personality of those pontiffs. Michelangelo was their master rather than their servant. All of them, however, except Pope Marcellus II, had high regard for Michelangelo as a person and as an artist, and Pope Marcellus reigned less than a month (April 9–May 1, 1555). Indeed, Pope Julius III is said to have remarked that if Michelangelo should die

before him, he would have the artist's body mummified so that
he might keep it always near him.

The remark is typical of the hysteria of the times of the
Counter-Reformation, the Catholic response to the spread of
Protestantism. Pope Julius III vigorously pursued this course of
religious reaction, which Pope Paul III had begun.

Michelangelo distrusted the exaggerated emotionalism of the
Counter-Reformation movement. Compared to the pure, simple
faith in Christ's love and mercy which he had learned from
Vittoria Colonna, the new trend of devotion to the forms rather
than the spirit of religion seemed superficial to him. Anony-
mous enemies, probably members of the Sangallo clique, accused him of heresy for having, like the marchesa, tried to find a
compromise between the Catholic and the Protestant interpretations of faith.

Wisely the Church did not press these charges; it preferred to
use Michelangelo's talents rather than to suppress them. But his
position made him feel isolated. He turned more and more to
the stability of architecture as a means of expressing his feelings
about the unity of man and God that he believed possible
through faith. His work on St. Peter's appeared to him his
testimony to that faith. He felt a spiritual compulsion to bring
that church to some final form.

Michelangelo's sculptor's hands, however, could not remain
idle. For relaxation from his exacting duties as chief architect of
St. Peter's, he took the marble capital from a column of an
ancient Roman temple, and in the privacy of his house, began,
about 1550, to fashion it into a *Pietà*.

The seven-and-a-half-foot-high group he produced, now
known as the *Duomo Pietà* because it eventually was placed in
the Cathedral (Duomo) of Florence, is actually a "Deposition."
It includes three figures besides the dead Christ—Nicodemus,
the Virgin, and Mary Magdalene—and represents them about

to prepare for burial the body of the Savior which has just been taken from the cross. The kindness and pity in the face of Nicodemus, who supports the body from the rear, is the key to the profound tenderness of the group. It is thought that this face is a self-portrait of Michelangelo, but more likely it is merely an expression of his religious feelings.

In his conversations in the cloister of San Silvestro, Michelangelo is reported by d'Ollanda to have said:

> In order to reproduce an even partial likeness of Our Lord, it is not enough to be a great painter. One must also lead an exemplary life and be as saintly as possible, so that the understanding may be directed by the Holy Ghost.

This echo of the preaching of Savonarola, which had so deeply affected Michelangelo in his youth, is evident in the *Duomo Pietà*. The pagan humanism, so incongruous in the *Christ* of Santa Maria sopra Minerva, is absent. Instead of a heroic nude athlete, this Christ is all spirit. Michelangelo seems to have discarded his delight in representing physical beauty and strength. Instead, the limp figure has a kind of radiance, as if the glow of inner light were shining through the physical frame.

Michelangelo deliberately left the surface of the three supporting figures rough. Hence they break up and diffuse the light that falls on the group. This treatment adds to the impression of transparency.

A flaw in the ancient marble caused the right arm of the Christ to break. (It has been patched and mended.) A similar mishap apparently deprived the sculptor of enough marble to carve the Virgin's left hand. Consequently, Michelangelo abandoned the work, and sold it. Unfortunately, the sculptor and architect Tiberio Calcagni, Michelangelo's young secretary,

The *Duomo Pietà* (Cathedral, Florence)

started to "finish" the group, and gave the Mary Magdalene an offensive high polish. But Calcagni died before he could extend his damage.

The *Duomo Pietà* is an expression in marble of the feelings about his spiritual destiny that Michelangelo put into a sonnet of 1554:

> Now hath my life across a stormy sea,
> Like a frail bark, reached that wide port where all
> Are bidden, ere the final reckoning fall
> Of good and evil for eternity.
>
> Now know I well how that fond fantasy
> Which made my soul the worshiper and thrall
> Of earthly art is vain; how criminal
> Is that which all men seek unwillingly.
>
> Those amorous thoughts which were so lightly dressed,
> What are they when the double death is nigh?
> The one I know for sure, the other dread.
>
> Painting nor sculpture now can lull to rest
> My soul, that turns to His great love on high,
> Whose arms to clasp us on the cross were spread.
>
> —tr. Symonds

Toward the end of the same year Michelangelo wrote to his nephew Lionardo in Florence: "As to my state of health, in view of my age I don't think I'm worse off than others of the same age." He was past eighty.

The grasping Lionardo had married, and his wife had presented him with an heir on April 14, 1554. Michelangelo had been much concerned with Lionardo's choice of a bride, but had approved his decision to take Cassandra Ridolfi. Their son continued the Buonarroti line until it became extinct in 1858.

At his advanced age, Michelangelo ate little and slept less. He claimed that a long sleep gave him a headache and an upset stomach. He would work on his sculpture by candlelight. In spite of being bothered by a painful bladder-stone, he exercised by riding horseback. He began, presumably for the first time in his life, to appreciate the quiet beauty of nature. After an escape to Spoleto, in September, 1556, to avoid physical harm from another invading army, he wrote: "Peace is not really to be found save in the woods."

Pope Paul IV sent messengers to summon Michelangelo back to Rome. Doubtless the pope feared that the artist might yield to Cosimo de' Medici, Duke of Florence, who was entreating Michelangelo to return to his city. Michelangelo was greatly flattered by this expression of loyalty on the part of a Medici, but he felt that he must continue his efforts on St. Peter's in Rome. He would gladly have left the emotionally and politically frantic atmosphere of Rome if it had not been for that obligation to his art and to his conscience.

Bramante had originally conceived the structure of St. Peter's as a Greek cross (that is, a cross of right angles and with arms of equal length) imposed upon a square, with four smaller crosses within the corners of the basic one. Semicircular apses were to terminate each arm of the basic cross. The great square space formed at the intersection of the arms of the basic cross was to be surmounted by a dome. The enormous stone piers (233 feet in circumference) at each corner of this center square had been built within three years of the cornerstone-laying in April, 1506.

From this core of masonry all other areas of the church had to grow outward, for each depended for stability on the buttressing power of those four piers. Consequently, the architects who followed Bramante could only add embellishments to his framework. During Sangallo's thirty years of direction, fundamental construction in the interior of the church had advanced to such a degree that it could not be altered. The central dome, how-ever, had not been started. Neither had the minor crosses in the corners of the basic cross, nor the hemispherical vaulting of the apses at the ends of the arms of that basic cross.

Michelangelo put his style on the interior simply by eliminat-ing Sangallo's confused system of corridors which would have resulted in a cluttering-up of the interior space with nonfunc-tional construction. These corridors, Michelangelo said, would make the church a shadowy lair for thieves, muggers, and rapists. One of his chief concerns was getting light into the building.

Fortunately not much of that labyrinthine elaboration had been built by the time of Sangallo's death. Michelangelo, therefore, could return the interior of the church to the clarity of Bramante's original plan. He surpassed that by getting rid of the projected four smaller crosses. Thus he produced one great cross-in-square which expresses the organic unity of the struc-ture and makes all movement within the church revolve around its core.

Michelangelo also eliminated Sangallo's plan for extending the eastern arm of the basic cross into an artificial nave with an elaborate facade, and for making entrances at the ends of the other arms. Instead, he designed a slight extension of the eastern end in the form of a porch with columns supporting a pediment. The peak of this pediment would have directed the spectator's eye toward the dome that could have been seen above it. This porch was to provide the only entrance to the church. Hence, the structure returned to its basic unity—one church instead of the two churches projected in Sangallo's design.

The actual work was accomplished by the *Fabbrica* of St. Peter's. This was a community of architects in which the older

St. Peter's, Rome. Rear view, showing most of Michelangelo's work

ones were partners and the younger ones students. Owing to his advanced age, Michelangelo had to direct this community by messages from his house at the opposite end of the city, a system that sometimes caused considerable confusion and at least one serious mistake.

Michelangelo concentrated his own efforts on devices for getting light into the enormous travertine (native stone) structure, and on designing the great dome. The incomplete state of the exterior walls of the church allowed him to design for them tiers of windows that not only admit plenty of light but also make the edifice seem to soar upward instead of imposing its tremendous weight on the ground. This aspiring quality of the outer frame is climaxed in the dome and its lantern, the peak of which is 435 feet above St. Peter's Square.

Michelangelo's dome is conceded to be the finest in the world. Its beauty comes from Michelangelo's harmonizing of force and repose. This produces a balance which is full of vigor. The lantern thrusts dramatically upward above the calm dome and produces an exalted conclusion to the mighty structure like the coda of a great symphony.

None of Michelangelo's designs was carried out exactly as he had made them. Nor did he live to see many of them actually executed. Lesser architects during the sixty years between Michelangelo's death and the consecration of St. Peter's imposed their ideas on his, and changing fashions in religion demanded alterations in the structure. St. Peter's today is by no means the wholly satisfactory edifice that Michelangelo might have made it.

XI: JOURNEY INTO
THE FUTURE

Because of Michelangelo's advanced age, his closest friends feared that those who would have to carry on his projects after his death would not grasp his conceptions fully enough from his drawings alone to realize them adequately. Consequently they urged him to make three-dimensional scale models for the guidance of his successors.

Loving secrecy about his works-in-progress as he did, Michelangelo was stubborn about exposing his unmastered ideas to criticism. Finally, however, he acknowledged the value of his friends' advice. In 1557 he began a clay model of the dome of St. Peter's, which he finished in wood in November, 1561. This, somewhat altered by Giacomo della Porta, one of Michelangelo's successors as chief architect of the basilica, may now be seen in the Sala dei Modelli (Hall of Models) at the foot of the dome itself.

At the same time (1558–59) Michelangelo also made a model of the staircase of the Laurentian Library in Florence. He had written to Vasari, on September 28, 1555, in answer to his friend's request for the design—Vasari was acting for Duke Cosimo de' Medici—that he was unable to remember what he had proposed to do with the stairs. "I recall a certain staircase, as it were in a dream," Michelangelo wrote, "but I do not think it is exactly what I thought of then [about 1533] because it is a clumsy affair, as I recall it."

The staircase that Bartolomeo Ammanati built from this clay model to connect the vestibule (1553) of the library with the reading room (1550) is probably the most startling of Michelangelo's architectural works. It is, perhaps, too overwhelming to be entirely satisfactory, for it almost wholly fills the small vestibule. That room, too high for its width, therefore seems choked. The visitor is uncomfortable in it, as if he too were being gagged by the overpowering flow of the staircase.

In the staircase Michelangelo seems to be anticipating the baroque style which was to follow him. This style broke with the straight lines and formal proportions of the classical Renaissance. For those it substituted curves and ovals, swirls and fantasies. Hence its name, "baroque" (literally "irregular; contrary to formal rules"). In spirit it reflects the highly emotional attitudes of the Counter-Reformation. Even in his old age Michelangelo could adapt himself to the feelings of his time. The Laurentian staircase is a "modern" departure from the stairway of the Palazzo Senatorio and from that of the Belvedere pavilion of the Vatican, which Michelangelo designed about 1550.

Persuasion from his friends in Florence to return to them continued to tempt Michelangelo to leave the intrigues of Rome. When his servant and companion Urbino died, after twenty-six years of devotion to the master, Michelangelo wrote to Vasari that he was now left "in this treacherous world with so many burdens . . . and nothing but unending wretchedness remains for me." But he felt too old to tear himself away from his house in Rome and his faithful Doctor Realdo Colombo, a famous physician, and he felt it would be a sin for him to abandon St. Peter's, where the drum of his dome was in process of construction.

Staircase of the Laurentian Library, Florence

He did, however, in 1559, consent to design the Church of San Giovanni dei Fiorentini (St. John the Baptist of the Florentines) in Rome, on the present Lungotevere dei Fiorentini, for his Florentine friends. This church had been begun by the Florentine Pope Leo X, and foundations were laid by Jacopo Sansovino, but it had been long since forgotten in spite of Michelangelo's having urged Pope Julius III to resume the construction.

Michelangelo's fingers were stiff. "Writing is extremely irksome to me—my hand, my sight, and my memory," he wrote in 1559. Still he produced four drawings for the Church of the Florentines, but he had to have them redrawn for Duke Cosimo by Tiberio Calcagni. The duke's commissioners chose the most elaborate of these proposals, but also the most compact. Possibly they liked it because it resembled the Baptistery in Florence. After many alterations in the design of the interior, the construction of the church was finally started by Giacomo della Porta in 1584, and completed by Carlo Maderna. The false facade was added in 1734 by A. Galilei.

The exterior, however, remained as Michelangelo conceived it—a circle set in a square. His sculptor's sense of form saw the exterior as a great cubic block from which the circular interior would emerge, as the St. Matthew emerges from the marble that imprisons him. This outer surface also solved the problem of locating the principal entrance to the church—a dilemma to previous architects of circular-plan structures.

Here, for the first time, Michelangelo emphasized mass itself rather than the piers, columns, and buttresses that combine to produce mass, as in the exterior of St. Peter's. Hence the design gives a strong expression of unity. Even the dome seems part of the structure itself rather than imposed upon it. The lighting is concentrated at the tops of the structural elements; hence, the aspiring quality of St. Peter's is reversed. In San Giovanni

Michelangelo's interest is in the terrific mass of masonry. It seems to express the religious feelings of his last years. The forms sink with the same resignation as those of the *Duomo Pietà*.

The few drawings that Michelangelo made for Cardinal Guido Ascanio Sforza for the Sforza Chapel of Santa Maria Maggiore show an extension of the same thinking that produced San Giovanni dei Fiorentini. Here Michelangelo was faced with the problem of adjusting a central-plan church to the longitudinal plan favored by the Counter-Reformationists. Those reactionaries thought that the perfection of a circle-square design was pagan in spirit. Such a plan was acceptable only for a church consecrated to a martyr, such as St. John the Baptist to whom San Giovanni dei Fiorentini was dedicated, for it followed the early Christian churches to the martyrs—for example, the fourth-century church of San Stefano Rotondo (Round St. Stephen's) on Rome's Celian Hill. Michelangelo harmonized these two ideas in the Sforza Chapel by omitting a dome and bringing the vaults of the conflicting areas—rectilinear altar-space and circular tomb-space (for the cardinal)—to a magnificent apex. Both areas are dramatized by remaining independent of each other below, but they are unified above. This solution greatly influenced the architects of the next generation.

After Michelangelo's death the actual building of the Sforza Chapel was begun by Tiberio Calcagni, and finished in 1573 by Giacomo della Porta. Both are more responsible than Michelangelo for the interior design and decoration.

Michelangelo's participation in the urban renewal of Rome, which had been in progress since the time of Pope Nicholas V (1447–55), did not end with his design for the remodeling of the Capitoline plateau into the Campidoglio. In 1558 he registered a plan for cleaning out the pit around the Column of

Trajan. This had become a city dump since 1536, when it was excavated in order to show off the sculptured monument for Charles V's triumphal entry. Twenty years' accumulation of garbage there, so near Michelangelo's house, finally provoked this move on his part; for, unlike Lorenzo the Magnificent, he had a keen sense of smell. But the authorities did nothing but approve the plan, even though Michelangelo offered to pay half the expense of executing it.

And in 1561 Michelangelo undertook to design an ornamental gate—the Porta Pia, now at the juncture of the Via XX Settembre and the Via Nomentana. This was to crown the redevelopment of the district into one of villas and gardens which Pope Pius IV wished to leave as a memorial to himself.

The structure Michelangelo designed combines the monumentality of a traditional—and practical—fortified entrance to a city with the frivolity of a stage setting. The latter was quite appropriate to the pleasure-palace region it was to be—and still is—and to the nonfunctional purpose of the gate. Drawings for only the central portal and for the cartouche (ornamental scroll-tablet) above it survive from Michelangelo's hand, but he undoubtedly directed his assistants in preparing plans for the rest of the gate.

The whole is a new conception of urban ornamentation. It is a medieval idea imposed upon a derivation of Roman antiquity. Hence it expresses, in the somewhat mixed-up vocabulary of the Counter-Reformation, the spirit of the times—half medieval, half something not yet fully determined in direction.

In the same year of 1561 a visionary Carthusian priest from Sicily, Antonio del Duca, finally prevailed, after twenty years of trying, on a pontiff to make a Christian church out of the ruins of the Baths of Diocletian, built in A.D. 305–6. In the sixteenth century these ruins contained a Carthusian convent; now they house the great National Museum. On August 5, 1561, Pope

Pius IV laid the cornerstone for this remodeling. The project was entrusted to the supervision of Michelangelo. He seems to have tackled it with the simplest possible solution, namely, to wall up the enormous main hall of the ruined baths and redecorate the interior. The result—the Church of Santa Maria degli Angeli (Virgin of the Angels), on Rome's Piazza Nazionale—was remodeled in 1749. It is now so different a conception from anything Michelangelo could have imagined that it is practically impossible to reconstruct his intentions.

Designs for others to execute were now almost all that the eighty-seven-year-old master had the strength to undertake. Among these was one for a bronze equestrian statue of King Henry II of France, commissioned by his widow, the former Catherine de' Medici, Lorenzo the Magnificent's great-granddaughter. Michelangelo's pupil Daniele da Volterra tried to execute this, but failed to satisfy the dowager queen. The horse was finally incorporated into Pierre Biard the Younger's statue of King Louis XIII.

Poor Daniele da Volterra was directed by Pope Pius IV to drape the nude figures in Michelangelo's *The Last Judgment* so that they would no longer offend the prudish tastes of the Counter-Reformation zealots. The commission earned Daniele the opprobrious nickname of "the breeches maker." Old as he was, Michelangelo was still capable of a typically acid reply to the pope's request for his permission to reform the fresco. "It is a small matter," he said, "to expurgate a painting, but a large one to straighten out the world, which is the proper business of Your Holiness."

As the winter of 1563 began, it became clear to Michelangelo's friends that his health was seriously failing. Yet he insisted on going outdoors in all kinds of weather, and on riding his chestnut pony. In his last letter, dated December 28, 1563, he told Lionardo: "I can't use my hand to write." Still, he kept working in secret on the great *Pietà* (called the *Rondanini Pietà*), now in the Castello Sforzesco, Milan, in a completely different style from anything Michelangelo had previously created. He was seen working on it four days before his death.

This unfinished, six-and-one-half-foot-high marble represents a standing Virgin supporting a dead, nude Christ. The figures are emaciated and attentuated. They are wholly spiritual, lost in feelings of resignation and renunciation. There is a fervent mysticism about the work—a deeply personal expression of feeling. Even if Michelangelo had lived, he could not have finished it; there was not enough marble. It was intended as a sketch—Michelangelo's final statement of his ultimate religious convictions—that the life of the spirit must be utterly detached from considerations of the flesh.

On February 14, 1564, Michelangelo suffered a stroke. Tiberio Calcagni found him wandering aimlessly in the rain, his speech incoherent. Calcagni forced him to go to bed, but Michelangelo would not stay there. He kept moving back and forth between an easy chair and the fireplace, complaining of fatigue. His dear friends—Calcagni, Daniele da Volterra, Tommaso dei Cavalieri—his servants, and his doctors stayed with him.

On February 18, Michelangelo made his will. It consists of only three sentences. His soul he left to God; his body to the earth; his material possessions to his nearest relatives. These three heirs were all he had ever truly cared about during his life. Then Cardinal Salviati was summoned to administer the sacraments to the obviously dying man. At a little before five o'clock on that Friday afternoon Michelangelo Buonarroti expired.

Michelangelo's body was taken to the Church of the Holy Apostles in Rome, not far from his house. There it lay in state, and there his funeral was celebrated. Pope Pius IV and all the

The *Rondanini Pietà* (Castello Sforzesco, Milan)

people of Rome intended to keep Michelangelo's remains in the crypt of the church.

Lionardo Buonarroti, however, arrived in Rome too late to see his uncle alive, but well aware that Michelangelo had wished to be buried in Florence. Lionardo had the body stolen, baled up like freight, and shipped to Vasari in Florence.

The city of Florence gave Michelangelo a magnificent public funeral. Then his body was laid in the parish church of his family, Santa Croce.

Lionardo tried to procure the *Duomo Pietà* to place above his uncle's final resting place, but its owner would not surrender it in spite of Michelangelo's wish to be buried beneath that group. Instead, Vasari executed a monument from marble donated by Duke Cosimo de' Medici. Vasari was not quite equal to this undertaking, and the memorial would have provoked a stinging comment from Michelangelo. Few persons pay much attention to it, however, preferring to remember Michelangelo by the majestic, awe-inspiring memorials of his earthly sojourn that he himself left to posterity.

CHRONOLOGY

Michelangelo's life	Michelangelo's major works
1475 Michelangelo Buonarroti born, Caprese (Caprese Michelangelo), March 6. Family returns to Florence, early April.	
1481 Mother, Francesca Buonarroti, dies, December 6.	
1485 Father marries Lucrezia Ubaldini. Michelangelo enters school of Francesco da Urbino.	
1488 Michelangelo apprenticed to Ghirlandaio workshop, April 1.	

Michelangelo's life	*Michelangelo's major works*
1489	Enters sculpture school in Medici garden under Bertoldo.	
1490	Joins household of Lorenzo de' Medici ("the Magnificent").	
1492	Death of Lorenzo the Magnificent, April 8. Michelangelo returns to father's house. Studies anatomy at Santo Spirito.	*Madonna of the Stairs* (Casa Buonarroti, Florence) *Battle of the Centaurs* (Casa Buonarroti) *Crucifix for Santo Spirito* (Casa Buonarroti)
1494	Flight from Florence to Bologna, Venice, and back to Bologna, October–November. Piero de' Medici exiled, November 9.	*Hercules* (lost) *St. Proculus* *St. Petronius*
1495	Michelangelo returns to Florence.	*Angel with Candlestick* (St. Dominic, Bologna)
1496	Arrives in Rome, June 24.	*St. John* (lost) *Sleeping Cupid* (lost)

Michelangelo's life	*Michelangelo's major works*
1501 Returns to Florence, spring. Contract with Cardinal Piccolomini, June 18. Commission for *David*, August 16; begins *David*, October 13.	*Bacchus* (Bargello) *Pietà* (St. Peter's) St. Peter St. Paul (Cathedral, Siena) St. Pius
1503 First poems.	
1504 *David* erected June 8. *Battle of Cascina* commissioned, August.	*David* (Academy, Florence) *Doni Holy Family* (Uffizi) *Taddei Madonna* (Royal Academy, London)
1505 Summoned to Rome by Pope Julius II, March. Commission for tomb of Julius II.	Bruges Madonna (Notre Dame, Bruges)
1506 Flees to Florence, April 17. Submits to pope, Bologna, November 29.	*Pitti Madonna* (Bargello) *St. Matthew* (Academy, Florence) *Pope Julius II* (lost)
1508 Returns to Florence, late February. Summoned to Rome, late March. Commission for Sistine Chapel ceiling, May 10; work begun, August.	

	Michelangelo's life	*Michelangelo's major works*
1512	Sistine Chapel ceiling unveiled to public, November 1.	Ceiling of Sistine Chapel (Vatican)
1513	Death of Pope Julius II, February 21. First contract with Della Rovere heirs for tomb of Julius II, May 6. Occupies house in Macello de' Corvi, Rome.	
1516	Second contract with Della Roveres, July 8. Commission for facade of San Lorenzo, October.	*Rebellious Slave* (Louvre) *Dying Slave* (Louvre) *Moses* (San Pietro in Vincoli, Rome)
1516 –20	Principally engaged in opening marble quarries in Pietra Santa (Seravezza district) and on designs for facade of San Lorenzo in Florence. Contract for facade canceled, March 10, 1520. Begins designs for Medici Chapel, November, 1520.	Four Slaves (Academy, Florence) *Christ* (Santa Maria sopra Minerva, Rome)

	Michelangelo's life	*Michelangelo's major works*
1529	Appointed director of Florence fortifications, April 29. Flees Florence for Venice, September 21; returns, late November.	
1530	Capitulation of Florence, August 12. Michelangelo in hiding. Pardoned by Pope Clement VII. Resumes work on Medici Chapel and Laurentian Library.	Tombs and *Madonna* (Medici Chapel) *Victory* (Palazzo Vecchio)
1532	Third contract with Della Roveres, April 29. Meets Tommaso de' Cavalieri.	*Apollo* (Bargello)
1534	Leaves Florence to live permanently in Rome, September. Pope Clement VII dies, September 25.	

	Michelangelo's life	*Michelangelo's major works*
1535	Commission for *Last Judgment*, April. Appointed member of Pope Paul III's household, and chief architect, painter, and sculptor to the Vatican, September 1.	
1536	Begins *Last Judgment*, May. Meets Vittoria Colonna.	*Last Judgment* (Sistine Chapel, Vatican) *Leah, Rachel* (San Pietro in Vincoli)
1538	Conversations at San Silvestro, October 13 and 20, and November 3. Begins designs for Campidoglio.	*Brutus* (Bargello)
1541	*Last Judgment* unveiled to public, December 25.	
1542	Fourth contract with Della Roveres ratified, November. Begins Pauline Chapel frescoes.	
1544	Serious illness, July–August.	*Conversion of St. Paul* (Pauline Chapel, Vatican)

Michelangelo's life	*Michelangelo's major works*
1545 Tomb of Julius II completed, February. *Conversion of St. Paul* finished, July.	
1546 Made citizen of Rome, March 20.	Cornice of Farnese Palace, Rome
1547 Appointed chief architect of St. Peter's, January 1. Death of Vittoria Colonna, February 25.	Designs for St. Peter's
1549 Death of Pope Paul III, November 10.	
1550 *Crucifixion of St. Peter* finished.	*Crucifixion of St. Peter* (Pauline Chapel, Vatican)
1556 Flight to Spoleto, September; recalled to Rome, October 31.	*Duomo Pietà* (Cathedral, Florence)
1560 Model of dome of St. Peter's completed. Designs for San Giovanni dei Fiorentini.	Work on St. Peter's

Michelangelo's life	*Michelangelo's major works*
1561 Designs for Porta Pia and Santa Maria degli Angeli.	
1563 Elected to Florentine Academy, January 31.	
1564 Michelangelo dies, February 18.	*Rondanini Pietà* (Castello Sforzesco, Milan)

BIBLIOGRAPHY

From the enormous number of books and articles about Michelangelo's life and works, the following have been selected for listing here principally because they are in English, are more or less readily available to the student, or are definitive works. The biography by Charles Holroyd contains a translation of Condivi's *Life of Michelangelo* and of d'Ollanda's transcription of the three conversations on art. There is no translation into English of the complete *Lives* of Vasari; the life of Michelangelo in the Penguin edition listed below is, however, adequate for the nonspecialist. Charles de Tolnay's five-volume biography of Michelangelo is currently available only in a large library or, if a copy can be located, at a high price.

I. Works by Michelangelo

Complete Poems and Selected Letters of Michelangelo, translated by Creighton Gilbert. New York: Random House, 1963, Modern Library.

The Letters of Michelangelo, translated by E. H. Ramsden. Stanford, Calif.: Stanford University Press, 1963, 2 vols.

II. Biography and Criticism

Ackerman, James S. *The Architecture of Michelangelo*. New York: Viking Press, 1961, 2 vols.

Clements, Robert J., editor. *Michelangelo, a Self-Portrait*. Englewood Cliffs, N.J.: Prentice-Hall, 1963.

Clements, Robert J. *Michelangelo's Theory of Art*. New York: New York University Press, 1961.

————. *The Poetry of Michelangelo*. New York; New York University Press, 1965.

Condivi, Ascanio. *The Life of Michelangelo Buonarroti*, translated by Herbert P. Horne. Boston: Merrymount Press, 1904.

Holroyd, Charles. *Michael Angelo Buonarroti*. New York: Charles Scribner's Sons, 1911.

Mariani, Valerio. *Michelangelo the Painter*. Milan: Arti Grafiche Ricordi, 1964.

Morgan, Charles H. *The Life of Michelangelo*. New York: Reynal, 1960.

Salmi, Mario, editor. *The Complete Work of Michelangelo*. New York: Reynal, 1967.

Symonds, John Addington. *The Life of Michelangelo Buonarroti*. New York: Random House (Modern Library), n.d.

Tolnay, Charles de. *The Art and Thought of Michelangelo*, translated by Nan Buranelli. New York: Pantheon, 1964.

————. *Michelangelo*. Princeton, N.J.: Princeton University Press, 1943–60. (I. The Youth of Michelangelo, 1943, 1947; II. The Sistine Ceiling, 1949; III. The Medici Chapel, 1948; IV. The Tomb of Julius II, 1954; V. The Final Period, 1960.)

Vasari, Giorgio. *The Lives of the Artists*, a selection translated by George Bull. Baltimore, Md.: Penguin Books, 1965.

Weinberger, Martin. *Michelangelo the Sculptor*. New York: Columbia University Press, 1967, 2 vols.

III. Background and History

Burckhardt, Jacob. *The Civilization of the Renaissance in Italy*. New York: Harper (Torchbooks), 1958, 2 vols.

Corvo, Frederick Baron (Frederick William Rolfe). *Chronicles of the House of Borgia*. New York: Dover, 1962.

Kristeller, Paul Oskar. *Renaissance Thought*. New York: Harper (Torchbooks), 1961.

Ridolfi, Roberto. *The Life of Girolamo Savonarola*, translated by Cecil Grayson. New York: Alfred A. Knopf, 1959.

Roeder, Ralph. *The Man of the Renaissance*. New York: Viking Press, 1935.

Schevill, Ferdinand. *The Medici*. New York: Harper (Torchbooks), 1960.

———. *Medieval and Renaissance Florence*. New York: Harper (Torchbooks), 1963, 2 vols.

Villari, Pasquale. *Life and Times of Savonarola*, translated by Linda Villari. New York: Charles Scribner's Sons, n.d.

Young, G. F. *The Medici*. New York: Random House (Modern Library), n.d.

INDEX

Adrian VI, 154

Alberti, Leon Battista, 14

Aldovrandi, Giovanfrancesca, 39, 41, 75

Alexander VI, 54, 82, 175

Ammanati, Bartolomeo, 220

Angel with Candlestick (San Domenico, Bologna), 41–44

Apollo (Bargello, Florence), 165–167

Apollo Belvedere, 55

Arca, Niccolò dell', 41

Aretino, Pietro, 179–180, 190

Arno River, 4–5

Atlas Slave (Academy, Florence), 142–148, 203

Awakening Slave (Academy, Florence), 142–148

Bacchus (Bargello, Florence), 46, 47–51, 64, 142

Baglioni, Malatesta, 157–158, 160–161

Bandinelli, Baccio, 162

Baptistery, Florence, 222

Baroque style, 220

Baths of Diocletian, remodeling of, 224–225

Battle of Anghiari (da Vinci), 67–71

Battle of Cascina, 70–71, 93

Battle of the Centaurs (Casa Buonarroti, Florence), 24–30, 70, 179

Bearded Slave (Academy, Florence), 142–148

Bentivogli, Giovanni, 39, 95

Bertoldo, Giovanni di, 16, 17, 18, 26, 74

Biard, Pierre, 225

Bible, 32

Bichiellini, Niccolò, 34

Bologna, Italy, 94, 95

Botticelli, Sandro, 23, 24, 59

Bracci, Francesco de', 197

Bramante, Donato, 82–83, 84, 91, 92, 97–98, 99–100, 103–104, 128, 203, 205, 215

Brancacci Chapel frescoes (Masaccio), 17

Brunelleschi, Filippo, 136, 151, 153

Brutus (Bargello, Florence), 182

Buonarroti, Buonarroto, 6, 9–10, 53, 54, 102, 106, 150, 157

Buonarroti, Cassandra, 5–6

Buonarroti, Francesca, 3, 5, 6

Buonarroti, Francesco, 4, 5–6

Buonarroti, Giovan Simone, 6, 150, 210

Buonarroti, Lionardo, 3, 12, 23, 46

Buonarroti, Lionardo (nephew), 157, 214, 225, 228
Buonarroti, Lodovico, 3–4, 5, 6, 8, 12, 18–19, 53, 54, 162
Buonarroti, Michelangelo
anatomical studies, 34
apprenticeship, 12–16
architect of St. Peter's, 204–205, 206, 211, 215–219, 220, 222
birth, 5
in Bologna, 38, 39–41, 75–76, 93–96
in Carrara, 80, 136–140
death, 226
director of Florence's fortifications, 157–160
early years, 9–10
education, 7, 10
foster-mother, 6
health, 197, 198
in Medici household, 16–31, 75, 150, 185
method of work, 89–91
poetry, 33, 75–76, 87–89, 105, 128, 162–163, 214
quoted, 6, 33, 73–75, 76, 83, 84, 87–89, 95, 98, 99, 101–102, 105, 106, 119, 123, 128, 138, 162–163, 180, 181, 186, 195–199, 204, 205, 210, 214, 219–220, 225
in Rome, 45–55, 77–84, 97–136
stepmother, 6–7, 53
in Venice, 38–39, 158
works of. See individual titles
Buonarroti, Sigismondo (Gismondo), 6, 210
Buoninsegni, Domenico, 140, 162

Calcagni, Tiberio, 212–214, 222, 223, 226
Campidoglio, 200–202, 206, 223
Capella Paolina, frescoes of, 196–197

Capponi, Niccolò, 156, 157–158
Caprese, Italy, 3, 4–5
Carrara, Italy, quarries of, 46–47, 80–81, 176
Cartoon, 67
Cavalieri, Tommaso de', 163, 165, 181, 202, 226
Cesena, Biagio da, 191
Charles V, Holy Roman Emperor, 156, 157, 199
Charles VIII, King of France, 38
Chiaroscuro, 66
Christ (Santa Maria sopra Minerva, Rome), 141–142, 148, 198, 212
Christianity, 20–21, 33, 34, 36, 117
Christ with the Woman of Samaria, 187
Church of San Lorenzo
facade, 135–136, 137, 138, 139–141, 148, 153
sacristy, 151–153
See also Medici Chapel
Church of Santa Maria degli Angeli, 225
Church of Santa Maria Novella (Florence), frescoes, 13
Classicism, 9, 19–20, 117
Clement VII, 154–155, 156, 157, 158, 161, 165, 174, 175, 176, 177–178, 210
Colombo, Realdo, 220
Colonna, Vittoria, 182–186, 187, 206, 211
Colonna family, 54
Commedia (Dante), 22
Condivi, Ascanio, 24
quoted, 14–15, 81, 133, 160, 174, 176, 178
Conversion of St. Paul, The (Capella Paolina, Vatican), 197, 209–210
Copernicus, 186
Cosimo, Piero di, 23, 59

Counter-Reformation, 185, 211, 220, 223, 224, 225
Credi, Lorenzo di, 59
Crucifix for Santo Spirito Monastery (Casa Buonarroti), 34–36, 142
Crucifixion, 187
Crucifixion of St. Peter, The (Capella Paolina, Vatican), 197, 206–209
Cupid (or *Apollo*), 46

Dante, 22, 24, 32, 41, 122, 182, 190, 191
D'Argenta, Piero, 94
David (Academy, Florence), 56–63, 67, 71, 77, 96, 133, 148, 162
Da Vinci, Leonardo. *See* Leonardo da Vinci
Dawn (Medici Chapel, Florence), 170
Day (Medici Chapel, Florence), 172
Dedel, Adrian, 154
Della Rovere, Francesco Maria, 135
Della Rovere, Giuliano, 79
Della Rovere family, 98, 126, 129, 136, 137, 154, 155, 161, 165, 176–177, 195–196
Dialogues (Francisco d'Ollanda), 185
Disegno, 16–17
D'Ollanda, Francisco, 185, 204
  quoted, 212
Donatello, 16–18, 56, 60
Doni, Angelo, 64
Doni Holy Family (Uffizi, Florence), 64–67, 73
Drawings, 163–165
Duca, Antonio del, 224
Duomo (Florence), 8, 23
Duomo Pietà (Duomo, Florence), 211–214, 223, 228
Dying Slave (Louvre, Paris), 131, 138, 198

Early Renaissance, 8–9
El Greco, quoted, 66
Etruscan sculpture, 14

Fabbrica, 216–218
Farnese, Alessandro, 175
Farnese Palace, 202–204
Ficino, Marsilio, 19, 20, 21
Fiesole, Mino da, 97
Flemish school of painting, 64
Florence, Italy, 3–4, 5, 7–9, 12, 16, 21, 22–23, 30, 31, 37, 38, 44, 53, 55–56, 60, 62, 63, 135, 156–161, 181–182
Franciotti, Galleoto, 83
Francis I, king of France, 198
Frizzi, Federigo, 141

Galilei, A., 222
Gallo, Jacopo, 46, 47, 83
Ghirlandaio, David, 12
Ghirlandaio, Domenico, 10–12, 13, 16, 29, 75
Ghirlandaio workshop, 10–11
Gianotti, Donato, 182
Giotto, 14
Giuliano de' Medici (Medici Chapel, Florence), 167, 168–172
Gonfalonier, 55
Gonzaga, Ercole, 176
Granacci, Francesco, 10–12, 15, 16, 22, 59
Greece, ancient, 9
Groslaye, Jean de Villiers de la, 46, 49

Head of a satyr, 17
Henry II, statue of, Michelangelo's design for, 225
Hercules, 36, 37, 44
Humanism, 9

Iliad (Homer), 22
Inferno (Dante), 190

Innocent VIII, 31–32
Intelletto, 89

Judaism, 117
Judith (Donatello), 60
Julius II, 54, 76–77, 79–85, 91, 92,
    93, 94, 95–96, 97, 98–99,
    101–102, 103, 104, 106, 125–
    126, 129, 135, 138, 150, 176,
    204, 210
    tomb of, 80–81, 84–85, 97, 98,
    126–127, 129, 135, 136, 141,
    148, 154, 155, 161, 175, 178,
    195, 197–198
Julius III, 210–211, 222

Landino, Cristoforo, 22
Laocoön, 55, 82, 131
Last Judgment, The (Sistine
    Chapel, Rome), 178, 180,
    187–195, 209, 225
Laurentian Library. See Medici Li-
    brary
Leah (San Pietro in Vincoli, Rome),
    196–197
Leda and the Swan, 165
Leo X, 128–129, 135–136, 137,
    138, 139, 140, 150–151, 153,
    154, 155, 175, 210, 222
Leonardo da Vinci, 56, 59, 62, 63–
    64, 66, 67–71, 73, 75
Lorenzo de' Medici (Medici Chapel,
    Florence), 167–170
Louis XIII, statue of, 225
Luther, Martin, 186

Maderna, Carlo, 222
Madonna (Medici Chapel, Flor-
    ence), 167, 172
Madonna and Child (Notre Dame,
    Bruges, Belgium), 71–73, 75,
    80
Madonna and Child with St. Anne
    (da Vinci), 63

Madonna of the Goldfinch (Ra-
    phael), 73
Madonna of the Stairs (Casa Buo-
    narroti, Florence), 24–29, 71,
    172
Man of the Renaissance, The (Roe-
    der), quoted, 179
Marcellus II, 210
Marcus Aurelius, statue of, 200–202
Masaccio, 14, 17
Medici, Alessandro de', 161–162,
    174, 181–182
Medici, Catherine de', 225
Medici, Cosimo de', 215, 219, 222,
    228
Medici, Giovanni de', 19, 38, 46,
    128–129
    See also Leo X
Medici, Giuliano de', 19, 136, 151
Medici, Giulio de', 129, 139–140,
    150–151, 153–154
    See also Clement VII
Medici, Lorenzino de', 182
Medici, Lorenzo de', 135, 136, 139,
    151
Medici, Lorenzo de' (the Magnifi-
    cent), 4, 7–8, 16, 17, 18–19,
    21, 22, 24, 30–32, 36, 37, 53,
    128, 136, 151, 224, 225
    academy of, 16, 19, 20–21, 24,
    32
Medici, Lorenzo di Pierfrancesco
    de', 44, 45
Medici, Piero de', 19, 36–37, 38,
    46, 135
Medici Chapel, 148, 154, 155, 156,
    161, 165, 167–174, 185, 204
Medici Library, 155, 156, 161, 219–
    220
Metamorphoses XII (Ovid), 26
Middle Ages, 51–52
Milan, Italy, 63
Milanesi, Baldassare del, 44, 45
Mirandola, Giovanni Pico della. See
    Pico

Montelupo, Raffaello da, 195, 198
Moscheroni, Alessandro, 71
Moscheroni, Giovanni, 71
Moses (San Pietro in Vincoli, Rome), 131–135, 138, 153, 176, 195, 198, 209

Neoplatonists, 20, 24
  See also Platonic Academy
Nicholas V, 223
Night (Medici Chapel, Florence), 165, 172

Orsini family, 54

Paganism, 33, 34, 36
Palazzo dei Conservatori, 199, 202
Palazzo Nuovo, 202
Palazzo Senatorio, 199, 200, 202, 220
Palazzo Vecchio, 59, 60, 148
Paul III, 175–177, 178, 179, 185, 187–188, 191, 192, 195, 197, 199, 200, 202, 204, 206, 210, 211
Paul IV, 210, 215
Perugino, Pietro, 59, 178
Peruzzi, Baldassare, 203
Petrarch, 41
Piccolomini, Francesco, 56
Pico della Mirandola, Giovanni, 19, 23
Pietà, 187
Pietà (St. Peter's, Rome), 46, 47, 49–52, 71, 148, 198
Piombo, Sebastiano del, 150
Pistoia, Giovanni da, 106
Pitti, Bartolommeo, 85
Pitti Madonna (Bargello, Florence), 85–87
Pius IV, 210, 224–225, 226–228
Plato, 19, 20, 31, 33
Platonic Academy, 20–21, 24, 32
Platonism, 185

Poliziano, Angelo, 19, 22, 23, 75, 179
Pollaiuolo, 16
Pope Julius II, 94–96
Porta, Giacomo della, 219, 222, 223
Porta Pia, Michelangelo's design of, 224
Pulci, Luigi, 22, 75

Rachel (San Pietro in Vincoli, Rome), 196–197
Raphael, 73–75, 82, 91, 103, 127, 128, 129, 203
Rebellious Slave (Louvre, Paris), 129–131, 198
Renaissance, 9, 117
  See also Early Renaissance
Riario, Raffaello, 44–46
Riccio, Luigi del, 181, 197, 198
Ridolfi, Cassandra, 214
Ridolfi, Niccolò, 182
Roman Forum, 199
Rome, Italy, 54–55, 81–82, 199–202, 223–225
  ancient, 9, 14
  sack of, 156, 186
Rondonini Pietà (Castello Sforzesco, Milan), 225–226
Rontini, Baccio, 195
Rubens, Peter Paul, 71

St. Gregory (Cathedral, Siena), 56
St. Matthew (Academy, Florence), 87, 89–90, 91, 93, 131, 142, 222
St. Paul (Cathedral, Siena), 56
St. Peter (Cathedral, Siena), 56
St. Peter's, restoration of, 79–80, 82–83, 103–104, 128, 202–203, 204–210, 211, 215–219, 220, 222
St. Petronius (San Domenico, Bologna), 39–44
St. Pius (Cathedral, Siena), 56

St. Proculus (San Domenico, Bologna), 39–44
Sangallo, Antonio da, 60
Sangallo, Antonio da, the Younger, 195, 202–203, 204, 205, 206, 215–216
Sangallo, Francesco da, 82
Sangallo, Giuliano da, 60, 76, 79, 82–83, 84, 91, 101, 102
San Giovanni dei Fiorentini, Michelangelo's designs for, 222–223
Sansovino, Jacopo, 222
San Stefano Rotondo, 223
Santa Croce, 228
Sanzio, Raphael. *See* Raphael
Savonarola, Girolamo, 21, 23–24, 31–32, 33, 37, 44, 55, 128, 212
Settignano, Italy, stone quarries of, 6
Sforza, Guido Ascanio, 223
Sforza, Lodovico, 63
Sforza Chapel of Santa Maria Maggiore, 223
Sibyls, 117
Signorelli, Luca, 75
Signoria, 3–4, 8, 31, 38, 55, 56, 67, 85, 92, 96, 158, 162
Sistine Chapel, frescoes of, 91, 97–125, 129, 131, 138, 154, 170, 176, 177–179, 187–195
cartoons for, 100–101
Sixtus IV, 79, 97, 126
Sleeping Cupid, 44–45
Soderini, Francesco, 93

Soderini, Piero, 55, 56, 62, 67, 92–94, 96, 135
Strozzi, Roberto, 198

Taddei, Taddeo, 73
Taddei Madonna (Royal Academy, London), 73
Terribilità, 62
Titian, 66, 179
Tondo, 64
Tornabuoni family, 13
Torrigiano, Pietro, 17–18, 63
Twilight (Medici Chapel, Florence), 170

Udine, Giovanni da', 174
Urbano, Piero, 141
Urbino, Francesco da, 10, 178, 197, 220

Valori, Baccio, 165
Varchi, Benedetto, 89
Vasari, Giorgio, 6, 14, 219, 220, 228
quoted, 15, 90, 103, 107, 127, 140, 188, 195
Venice, Italy, 7, 16
Verrocchio, Andrea, 16
Victory (Palazzo Vecchio, Florence), 148
Volterra, Daniele da, 225, 226

Western Hemisphere, discovery of, 186

Young St. John the Baptist, 44
Young Slave (Academy, Florence), 142–148